Walking Welsh History

Walking Welsh History

A HISTORY OF SOUTH AND MID-WALES ON FOOT

Rebecca Deakin

First published in Great Britain in 2025 by
PEN AND SWORD HISTORY
An imprint of
Pen & Sword Books Ltd
Yorkshire – Philadelphia

Copyright © Rebecca Deakin, 2025

ISBN 978 1 39907 960 0

The right of Rebecca Deakin to be identified as Author of this work has been asserted by her in accordance with the Copyright, Designs and Patents Act 1988.

A CIP catalogue record for this book is available from the British Library.

All rights reserved. No part of this book may be reproduced, transmitted, downloaded, decompiled or reverse engineered in any form or by any means, electronic or mechanical including photocopying, recording or by any information storage and retrieval system, without permission from the Publisher in writing. NO AI TRAINING: Without in any way limiting the Author's and Publisher's exclusive rights under copyright, any use of this publication to 'train' generative artificial intelligence (AI) technologies to generate text is expressly prohibited. The Author and Publisher reserve all rights to license uses of this work for generative AI training and development of machine learning language models.

Typeset in Times New Roman 11/14.5 by
SJmagic DESIGN SERVICES, India.
Printed and bound in the UK by CPI Group (UK) Ltd, Croydon, CR0 4YY.

The Publisher's authorised representative in the EU for product safety is Authorised Rep Compliance Ltd., Ground Floor, 71 Lower Baggot Street, Dublin D02 P593, Ireland.
www.arccompliance.com

For a complete list of Pen & Sword titles please contact:
PEN & SWORD BOOKS LIMITED
George House, Units 12 & 13, Beevor Street, Off Pontefract Road,
Barnsley, South Yorkshire, S71 1HN, England
E-mail: enquiries@pen-and-sword.co.uk
Website: www.pen-and-sword.co.uk

or

PEN AND SWORD BOOKS
1950 Lawrence Rd, Havertown, PA 19083, USA
E-mail: uspen-and-sword@casematepublishers.com
Website: www.penandswordbooks.com

Contents

Introduction vi

Chapter One   Dylan Thomas and the Uplands in Swansea,
                   and Laugharne in Carmarthenshire 1
Chapter Two   Muriel Drinkwater and Penllergaer 17
Chapter Three   My Favourite Castles of South Wales 32
Chapter Four   Kilvey Hill 113
Chapter Five   Swansea and Copper 123
Chapter Six   The Rebecca Riots 161
Chapter Seven   Swansea Docks 175
Chapter Eight   One of my Favourite Finds 186

Bibliography 192
Index 194

Introduction

As far back as I can remember I have always loved history.

I am a graduate from Swansea University, where I obtained a BA Hons degree in Ancient History.

A couple of people when I told them that I wanted to study history remarked that they find the subject boring or queried what is the point in looking backwards and what could we do with this knowledge.

But I strongly believe that there is so much to learn from the past and that the things we know or do today are firmly rooted in the past.

I find all of history interesting, but I especially love researching an event or a place, untwisting the tangled haze and learning about the people it directly affected. I am particularly interested in obscure people of history, such as the working class, women of history and minorities, as they have not always been fully recorded or represented within history.

The more you delve into this book, the clearer this will become.

To me, when I learn about history, I treat it like a story and it paints a picture in my mind. It comes to such life when I can stand in an actual place and know its past, treading in the footsteps of people who have gone before.

I am acutely aware that there can be biased sources, and that history needs to be analysed and evaluated to reach a conclusion. Something that I love to do.

It will always remain my passion and this book is a demonstration of many of the places I've visited, whether it be in search of something,

Introduction

following directions or discovering landscapes and finding things – Second World War planes, for example.

I have loved everywhere I've visited, and each time I learn something new, it rapidly becomes my latest obsession. This book will demonstrate a few of my key favourites and mention some people of history that I have found to be captivating. Of course, I have researched deeper into these characters.

My other passion is the great outdoors. I love getting outside and exploring new places. I find this rewarding and beneficial for my physical and mental wellness.

It is a major bonus for me that I can combine two of my passions into one hobby. Every place is a new adventure to explore with a different story to tell.

It really brings history alive for me, to be able to stand in the very place where it all happened.

I am a natural overthinker and the skills that served me so well during my degree, such as analysing and evaluating, can spill into day-to-day life a little too much when not necessarily needed. My mind is often racing and can be hard to silence.

I see all possibilities and all sides of things which is an important skill set for when a problem needs solving, although not so much when you are simply trying to relax and recharge.

I find that walking is really beneficial, helping to slow my mind down, perhaps because walking requires me to be physically active and uses my cognitive function to concentrate on what my body is doing, but also there are new things to see, or sounds to hear that in turn centre and focus my attention.

This book will hopefully encourage you to get out there and explore, and provide introductions into some of my favourite Welsh history.

CHAPTER ONE

Dylan Thomas and the Uplands in Swansea, and Laugharne in Carmarthenshire

Utter the words 'Rage, rage against the dying of the light' to people, especially the Welsh, and in particular people living in Swansea, and there is an extreme likelihood that they will reply with 'Do not go gentle into that good night'. These are the opening words from the famous poem *Do not go gentle into that good night* written by arguably Swansea's most illustrious poet: Dylan Thomas.

> Do not go gentle into that good night,
> Old age should burn and rave at close of day;
> Rage, rage against the dying of the light.

Thomas is considered to be one of the best Welsh poets of all time, even though he only wrote in English. Some of his other most famous works include *Under Milk Wood*, *A Child's Christmas in Wales* and a *Portrait of the Artist as a Young Dog*.

He led a turbulent and interesting life. He was born in my home town, in fact within easy walking distance from my childhood home. This has led

A wood carving of the poet Dylan Thomas in Cwmdonkin Park.

me to be immersed in his works, but also stories about his personal life. Some of these stories may be exaggerated or imagined. Some regard him as an important wordsmith, others may regard him as a drunk. This already suggests him to be an interesting character and hence what drove me to learn more about him.

I have also grown to appreciate his writing. I enjoy his theatrical style, rawness and the way he is able to paint a picture in my mind.

The Uplands is a community within Swansea, South Wales. It is deeply rooted in Thomas' life, having been born there and where he wrote some of his published works.

Thomas loved his hometown of Swansea and even though he would later move around between Laugharne, Newquay, London and even travelling with his work as far as New York, Swansea, I believe, still held an important place in his heart. In a 1943 radio broadcast, Thomas would speak of his home town stating: 'by the side of a long and splendid evolving inshore the sea town was my world'. Swansea would later grow in its own right and become a city.

Thomas was born to parents David John and Florence Hannah Thomas. His father worked at the local grammar school as an English literature professor and perhaps this is where Thomas inherited his love of language.

At school, it is said, Thomas was intellectually lazy in regard to any subject that did not interest him. However, his knowledge of the English language and poetry was grand.

Thomas' mother was the daughter of a farmer. Thomas would often go on holiday to his grandfather's country home and in his poem *Fern Hill* he would recount all of its wonders.

He began writing his poetry young, and had work published by his teens. He had a true love of words, their rhythm, their sound and the way they can be used for multiple meanings.

Thomas left school at the age of sixteen and became a journalist for the *South Wales Evening Post*, although this was brief and Thomas would become a freelance writer.

In 1934 when Thomas was twenty, he moved to London. It was whilst there that he won the Poets' Corner Prize, and his first book consisting of eighteen poems was published. This book was a collection from his poetry notebooks that he had written years earlier and it received vast literary acclaim.

Thomas was not really concerned with discussing any social or intellectual issues within his writing. He was much more focused on lyricism and emotion, reasons why I personally enjoy his works.

It was whilst in London that he would meet his future wife.

In 1937 on 11 July, Thomas married Caitlin McNamara, a dancer. They were extremely poor and did not have the blessings of their parents.

Thomas is as much famous for his writing as for his turbulent lifestyle. Caitlin was perhaps not only his wife, but also his drinking partner.

Their marriage is alleged to have been a stormy one, full of alcohol and infidelity. Caitlin in her memoirs would say 'ours was not a love story, it was a drink story'.

After they wed, they lived with relatives who were reluctant to host them. They then moved into a borrowed house in the fishing village of Laugharne in Carmarthenshire, Wales.

This house would become their main address, although the couple lived in various temporary homes in England and Wales during and after the Second World War, up until Thomas' passing in 1953.

Although Thomas was appreciated during his lifetime as a writer, this was perhaps more in literary circles and he would find earning money from writing quite difficult. He would add to his income with radio broadcasts and reading tours. By the late 1940s, his radio work would bring him into public attention, having featured often by the BBC as an accessible voice.

One of my favourite walks concerning Thomas, begins at his first school, housed at 22 Mirador Crescent, Uplands, SA2 0QX. Thomas turned the lane behind the school into 'the lane of confidences', where he told schoolfriends he could grow wings and fly over the roof tops of Swansea. Standing outside number 22, continue along Mirador Crescent, turn right at the end of the street, then left following the pavement all the way up to Cwmdonkin Drive. It is here that you will find the house where Thomas was born in an upstairs front bedroom.

He spent around twenty-three years living there and it is where he wrote two-thirds of his work.

Born on 27 October 1914, I wonder if his parents could have guessed that he would go on to be one of Wales' most famous writers and poets.

By 2003, this house had become a bedsit and needed work, despite its past famous occupant. Fortunately, an Uplands local, Geoff Haden, took over the house and lovingly restored and furnished it as it would have looked during Thomas' childhood.

The house now stands as a monument to the famous writer, looking almost as if Thomas had just popped out for milk and bread and would be back home at any moment.

There is a circular blue plaque to commemorate the writer on the wall of the house, near the front door, and beneath it is the same in the Welsh language.

The house is open to the public for house tours every Wednesday and Sunday. According to their website, they pride themselves on being welcoming and have guides ready to greet you and provide visitors with an insight to the house's history and of course to the man himself.

Visitors are also then able to roam the house freely, having the chance to see Thomas' bedroom as it would have been in around 1934.

A plaque announced Dylan Thomas' birthplace at 5 Cwmdonkin Drive, Swansea.

Prices for tours start from £8 per adult and booking must be made in advance.
Telephone number: 01792472555
Email address info@dylanthomasbirthplace.com

House tours are not all that this house can offer. You can also attend an afternoon tea, including home-baked pastries, scones, tea cakes and sandwiches or an Edwardian-style dinner, that's accompanied by a phonogram, a piano and games in a style typical of the times.

The house even boasts visits from the then Prince Charles (now King Charles III) and actor Johnny Depp, who would say, 'I think it's gonna stick with me for a while' after visiting the house.

Dylan Thomas's birthplace.

Across the road from the house is where I continue my walk, to a bench that boasts a quote from Thomas' poem *The Hunchback in the Park*: 'Drinking water from the chained cup'.

Continuing past the bench through Clevedon Court, you will see railings that will lead you down into Cwmdonkin Park. This is via a concrete slope and therefore would be accessible for pushchairs and wheelchairs.

It was in this park where Thomas would play as a young child and it would later become a great inspiration for some of his works, such as *The Hunchback in the Park* which starts:

> A solitary mister
> Propped between trees and water

From the opening of the garden lock
That lets the trees and water enter
Until the Sunday sombre bell at dark

Eating bread from a newspaper
Drinking water from the chained cup
That the children filled with gravel
In the fountain basin where I sailed my ship
Slept at night in a dog kennel
But nobody chained him up

This poem speaks of a disfigured man in solitude in a park being teased by the children and trying to stay clear of the park keeper. There is a stark contrast between the cruel taunting the man endures and the beauty of the park. I believe the poem teaches us about kindness.

A wooden plaque on the railings leading down into Cwmdonkin Park, pointing out a link to Dylan Thomas.

The sun beaming through Cwmdonkin Park.

A Victorian creation, the park was opened in the summer of 1874. It was built on what was Cwmdonkin reservoir and two fields that were purchased from the state belonging to James Walker, a local landowner. The park boasts beautiful scenery from pretty flowerbeds to sky-reaching trees. There is a play area for children, a bowling green, a tennis court and a small café named after the man himself: Dylan's.

In 1963, a memorial stone was placed in the park, reciting these lines from Thomas' *Fern Hill*: 'Oh as I was young and easy in the mercy of his means time held me green and dying though I sang in my chains like the sea.'

Dylan Thomas and the Uplands in Swansea

Above: Trees at Cwmdonkin Park.

Right: A plaque commemorating the opening of Cwmdonkin Park in 1874.

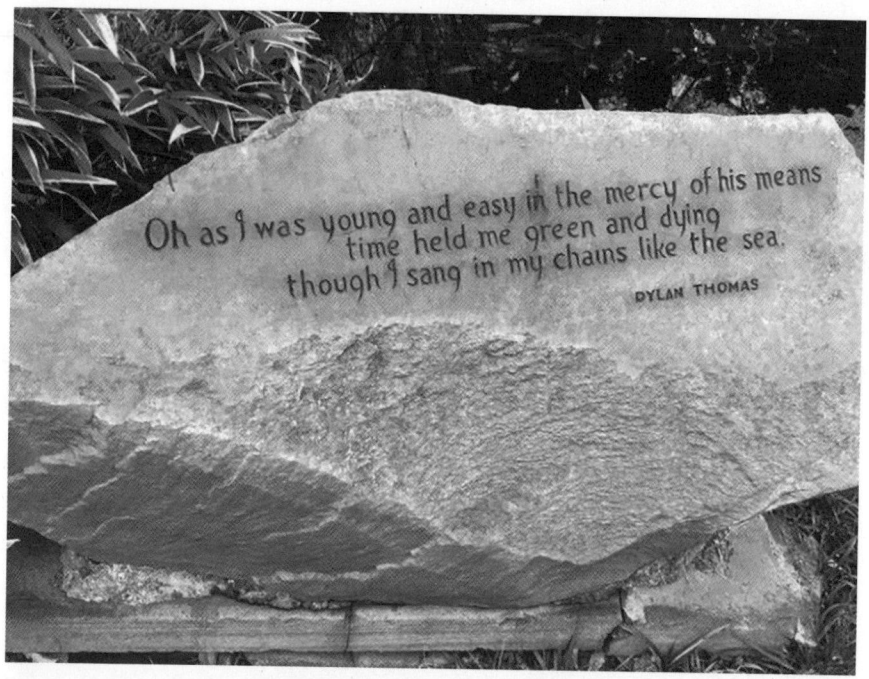

A memorial stone quoting lines from the poem Fern Hill by Dylan Thomas. This stone can be found at Cwmdonkin Park.

If you exit the park through the gate opposite this stone, make your way straight down, crossing the road and following the curved hill to Uplands Crescent, you'll find where I end my walk: Uplands Tavern.

In Thomas' day it was called the Uplands Hotel, and is known to have been his local watering hole. Perhaps this is where he discovered his love of bars and beer ...

Another of my favourite walks concerning Thomas is in South Wales. While he loved his hometown of Swansea, Thomas would also grow to have a special relationship with a place in Carmarthenshire called Laugharne and on visiting there, I can see why. He would end up living here off and on for almost two decades, resulting in many Dylan Thomas hotspots here.

Thomas visited Laugharne for the first time in 1934. He and Caitlin first lived in rooms at Castle House on Market Street, as he knew the owner, Richard Hughes. Here he would write in the gazebo overlooking the estuary.

The Thomases did not stay long in their rooms at Castle House, the married couple would move into Fisherman's Cottage at Eros, 2 Gosport Street. At the time of living there, there was no plumbing and they would have had to trek down the hill to fetch water from a public tap. They lived here for around six months.

Whilst there, Thomas sent a letter to James Laughlin, his American publisher, in which he describes Laugharne as 'a very odd town' and that it was 'undiscovered by painters because the sea is mostly mud nobody knows when the water will come in or out or where it comes from anyway.' He would also describe it as a sociable place, with of course some decent pubs in the area.

One of these pubs was the Cross House Inn.

The older residents of the village recall memories of the famous writer at the pub, cradling a beer and writing on the back of cigarette packets, just for them to be cleared by the staff and thrown away.

In need of money, Thomas sent a letter to Augustus John, writing 'see you on the cross,' although macabre, it was also a reference to the pub.

Thomas' next place of residency would be Sea View, owned by friends of his and Caitlin, Ivy and Ebie Thomas. By this time, the married couple were expecting their first child.

The couple had happy times here, but unfortunately their debts to local businesses became too great, so together they made a dart for Hampshire to Caitlin's mother. Although Thomas still wished to return to his beloved Laugharne, the couple could not find a new place to live there and so in 1944 they moved to Newquay, South Wales.

As a result, Newquay has also become a hotspot for Dylan Thomas enthusiasts.

It is believed by some that he took inspiration from this town and its locals for his work *Under Milk Wood* and started writing it during his stay there.

Thomas drew a sketch of a fictional place, which some would argue looks a lot like Newquay, but not the locals of Laugharne as some there have long claimed their village as the inspiration.

It has never been fully revealed where the poem was based and perhaps it could even have been a mix of the two. Having visited Newquay and

Laugharne, both are beautiful places that could easily have inspired Thomas in his writing of the poem.

The couple rented a bungalow called the Majoda and while cold and draughty, it had gorgeous views of the bay.

Their neighbour was a lady called Vera Killick, living with her daughter whilst her husband William was away serving. Caitlin and Vera became close, possibly driving Dylan out.

Captain Killick returned home after his mission at war, understandably exhausted and stressed. Perhaps he was not too impressed by his wife's friendship with their hippy, non-serving neighbours. He may have even felt excluded and possibly jealous.

Events would come to a head on 6 March 1945. Thomas had been meeting John Eldrige and Fanya Fisher, two London film colleagues, who were staying at the Black Lion public house in Newquay. Whilst drinking in The Commercial, they would encounter Captain Killick. A heated exchange took place between them, with Killick verbally attacking Thomas and his friends in a hostile discussion about the war. They would clash again that very same evening in the Black Lion pub, but this time a more physical exchange took place. This was broken up and Thomas along with his friends would return to the Majoda.

However, Killick would return home to arm himself with weapons, one of which was a machine gun. He then proceeded to attack the Majoda.

As a result, Killick would be tried for attempted murder. He was acquitted, as he had had an exemplary military record and his state of mind after his time serving was taken into account.

These events would be later dramatized in a film *The Edge of Love* starring Keira Knightley, Sienna Miller, Matthew Rhys and Cillian Murphy.

It was from this residence that the couple would move back to Laugharne into the Boathouse and that now notorious writing shed.

This move only happened due to an extremely kind benefactor, Margaret Taylor, a lover of Thomas' works, who funded the money for the couple to live there rent free.

Thomas would write of his appreciation in a letter to Margaret: 'For this place I love and where I want to work ... this is it: the place, the house, the workroom, the time. All I shall write in this water and tree room on the cliff, every word will be my thanks to you. You have given me a life and I'm now going to live.'

It was in the 1950s that Thomas travelled to America. Whilst he was gaining a degree of fame there, his relationship with alcohol and his erratic nature were worsening.

It was on his fourth visit to New York in 1953 that Thomas became drastically ill and would end up falling into a coma. He sadly passed away on 9 November. His body would be returned to Wales and he would later be laid to rest on 25 November 1953 at St Martin's churchyard in his beloved Laugharne, Carmarthenshire.

When Thomas passed away, his widowed mother moved into the Boathouse. She was so proud of Thomas and enjoyed people coming round wanting to talk about him.

The Boathouse is now a museum with a shop and tearoom.

The writing shed, just above the Boathouse and in similar style to Thomas' birthplace, still stands just waiting for his return with a jacket swung over a chair. The desk is cluttered with pens and papers, awaiting the author's arrival.

The furniture is not the original as belongings were sold by Caitlin for money after Thomas' death, but you can still get that true sense of the writer.

The shed, originally a wooden garage, was erected in the 1920s to house Laugharne's first motorcar, a Wolseley belonging to a resident who was staying in the Boathouse that summer.

By 1949 the garage was converted into Thomas' writing shed, with the additions of windows, furniture and a stove.

The original blue doors have been removed and replaced with duplicates, but you can see the originals on display at the Dylan Thomas Centre in Swansea.

After he died, Thomas' body was taken to Pelican House in Laugharne, where his parents had once lived after he moved them there in 1949. He would often call in on them, stopping by to do the crossword with his father.

There is a story that alleges when his coffin was brought back on board a liner, sailors played cards upon it and when Caitlin came across them below deck, she would even end up dancing on it.

Once it had arrived on British soil, the coffin eventually reached Laugharne after a detour via Cornwall, but it was too large to fit through the front door of Pelican House and had to go through the window instead.

The Browns Hotel of Laugharne was another favourite. After moving to the area, Thomas would pop in at the pub most mornings for breakfast and tea, and could usually be found back there most nights drinking, joined by his wife. The landlords of Sea View, Ivy and Ebie Thomas, were also the owners of Browns Hotel.

He was such a regular that he would hand out the Browns' telephone number as his own.

Perhaps the pub had acted as some inspiration for *Under Milk Wood*, whilst he sat listening to tales and conversations of the locals. I have visited this pub myself and many a picture of Thomas adorns the walls there.

I've had the privilege to visit his grave, where it has become a custom for people to leave pennies or coins, perhaps in sympathy for his penniless life and how he is still owed for his literary works that are still being enjoyed to this day.

His grave is extremely plain, just a white wooden cross that is replaced every once in a while. Although rather simple there is beauty in its simplicity. Caitlin is also buried at the church, even though after Thomas' passing she moved to Italy and had another partner and child.

It was whilst on a book tour in Laugharne in the eighties that she spoke to the vicar there and arranged to be buried here when her time came. Her name is on one side of the cross while Thomas' is on the other.

Within Laugharne there is a route called Dylan Thomas Birthday Walk. The path was originally created and paid for by the Laugharne Corporation in 1856 as a way for cocklers and locals to be able to walk to their share of the cocklebeds on the lower and upper marshes when high tide prevented other routes.

This pathway would provide Thomas with inspiration for *Poem in October*.

On visiting Laugharne I could easily see why Laugharne stole a piece of Dylan's heart.

I visited on a quiet weekday with sun shimmering high above Laugharne Castle. It was as if I stepped into a storybook away from the outside world.

There was beauty at every corner, from the towering castle standing guard over the estuary, to the friendly locals and quaint buildings.

I loved my first visit to Laugharne so much that I would return the next year on my thirtieth birthday to follow the footsteps that Thomas took on his thirtieth birthday along the path mentioned above.

These footsteps are recorded in what has become one of my favourite works by Thomas – *Poem in October*.

It reminds me to appreciate things as he describes what he sees and at the end of poem there is the hope to still be here next year. This spoke to me.

> And there could I marvel my birthday
> Away but the weather turned around. And the true
> Joy of the long dead child sang burning
> In the sun.
> It was my thirtieth
> Year to heaven stood there then in the summer noon
> Though the town below lay leaved with October blood.
> O may my heart's truth
> Still be sung
> On this high hill in a year's turning.

Throughout the poem, Thomas describes what he sees. Along the birthday walk, there are informative panels at different places with the stanzas of the poem on them, and as you read you can look out at what Thomas would have seen. For example, I remember reading the line 'and this castle brown like owls' and in my view to the distance stood Laugharne Castle.

This was amazing to me as although the poem is vivid in its descriptions, the fact that I could see the things that inspired Thomas really allowed me to feel that I was walking in his footsteps.

The starting point of this work is at Laugharne Harbour carpark and is clearly signposted.

The route is approximately two miles (3.2km) and follows a muddy incline. At the very top you are surrounded by spectacular views

The last panel containing the last verse describes Thomas' hope to be there this time next year and the panel invites you to make this birthday walk your own, reciting out loud the last verse of the poem and replacing Thomas' age with your own.

I was even able to gain some free chips and a pint from the local establishments for reciting a few lines of the poem on my visit as it was my birthday.

Years on after his death both Thomas' works and reputation still persevere, and whatever you may think of him, to quote the man's own words, he certainly did not 'go gentle into that good night'.

Dylan Thomas art found on a bench at Cwmdonkin Park.

CHAPTER TWO

Muriel Drinkwater and Penllergaer

In Penllergaer Forest while the dog walkers walk, the people stroll and the runners run between the many tall towering old trees, the wind whistles through the rustling leaves, whispering the story of young Muriel Drinkwater, the schoolgirl who never returned home.

This chapter and these walks are perhaps not for the faint-hearted, but when I was told that someone was murdered here in the 1940s, my inquisitive historian mind switched on and I could not help but do a little research.

Penllergaer Forest does have some pretty walks, including three main loops through the forest and neighbouring Tircoed Forest Village from around twenty minutes to an hour. There is a carpark at Penllergaer Forest and some short trails from there.

For this walk, we didn't follow a route, but just explored, with the aim to include the old railway tracks. It was autumn time so a bit muddy, but I always love the orange colours that are everywhere that time of year.

This torrid tale begins at Tyle Du Farm where the Drinkwater family once lived, including young Muriel who was born in the summer of 1933. She was the youngest of four children and lived with her parents Percy and Margaret. She was very intelligent and attended the local grammar school at Gowerton.

The trees of Penllergaer Forest.

This photograph is of an overgrown area , where it is believed that Muriel's house once stood.

Muriel was known as the nightingale and was often singing and skipping around the place; a very happy child. On the fatal day of 27 June 1946, Muriel was dropped off by the school bus, to take her usual route home, just as she had done many a time.

Her path home from the bus stop would have been much more remote than it is today as the area now boasts a motorway, a service station and a housing estate. She had to walk through the forest to get home, a quiet walk taken often by her and her sisters.

At around 4:30pm her mother Margaret while making a pot of tea saw her daughter about 400m away. Muriel then weaved into the trees out of sight along the path. Sadly she would never make it home for that cup of tea and this would cruelly be the last time her mother saw Muriel alive.

'She lost sight of her for a few moments,' said former detective inspector Paul Bethell in the BBC documentary *Dark Land: Hunting the Killers*.

Muriel was pulled from the path into the woodlands, attacked, raped and murdered in the undergrowth of the Penllergaer Forest, just a short distance from her mother and safety.

Although Penllergaer has changed over the years, the tragedy of this crime still casts a veil over the area.

Along the path before her brutal attack, Muriel was passed by young Hubert Hoyles, thirteen years of age, who had just been at the Drinkwater farm to buy some eggs from Muriel's mother. The two children spoke briefly and then continued their separate ways, unaware that Muriel was strolling towards her violent death and that suspicion would surround Hubert for a large part of his life.

When Muriel did not arrive home, her mother was not too worried at first, assuming her daughter had just gone off to play. However, after some time had passed the worry started to set in and a search party was put together. Muriel's father and some other locals began looking for her.

The area, lit up by glowworms, would have echoed with the cries of her parents as the search party was in vain.

However, it was only the following day that the gruesome crime was fully discovered. On finding her body lying in some undergrowth, PC David Lloyd George let out a piercing blast on his police whistle.

A path through Penllergaer Forest.

Penllergaer Forest.

Muriel had been brutally beaten around her head and shot twice in her chest at point-blank range. Reports say that she had one arm raised and her eyes wide open.

South Wales Evening Post said the spot in which she was found had 'patches of fern and brambles in which a man may sink out of sight'. The gun used, a Colt 45 American army pistol made at Springfield Armoury in 1942 and then sent out to Europe, was found tossed in the nearby undergrowth.

During the war American servicemen were stationed at Penllergaer and it was thought that one of them had sold the gun to someone else. Posters of the gun were spread around, including being shown in cinemas in a hope of tracing an owner or some information, but this was unfortunately unsuccessful.

The bludgeon weapon that was used was never found.

Cigarette ends and sweet wrappers were also found at the site, suggesting that the killer had being lying in wait for his victim to innocently walk by.

Hubert, who had seen Muriel on her way home, was taken in for questioning. He told police that a few weeks earlier he had seen a man on that path, a man in his thirties with a local accent. He described him as well-dressed with thick and fluffy hair. He had appeared to Hubert from behind the bushes and had asked Hubert where he was going and what he was doing, before telling him to get going.

At a later date, Hubert would say about meeting the strange man, quite possibly the killer that 'I can't be certain but it was some coincidence that he happened to be there at that spot so soon before the murder because in all the years of going up and down that path I never saw another soul.'

Even though a description of the man was released, and visits were paid to every man within a 400m square radius and interviews of over 20,000 men living in the South Wales area took place, no killer could be found.

The case eventually went cold, but years on people in the local community still talked about it. Some possibly suspected Hubert, but another person some suspected was a man called Harold Jones. No-one really knew who was behind it or who could be hiding the truth and that must have left a horrible sense of uncertainty and unease within the community.

At just fifteen years of age in 1921 Harold Jones had murdered eight-year-old Freda Burrell in Abertillary.

Even though Jones was arrested the locals believed him to be innocent, and that he had been framed by detectives from London. After being acquitted of the charge, Jones was paraded through the town upon the shoulders of the locals. But devastatingly just days later he went on to murder Freda's friend, Florence Little. He then confessed to both murders, giving a 'desire to kill' as his reason. He was not sentenced to death as he was under sixteen years of age at the time.

He was instead sent to jail for twenty years. He would later go on to join the army and came back to Wales a mere four months before Muriel's shocking murder.

There was no evidence to place Jones at the scene. He died of cancer in 1971.

These events truly had rocked the community of Penllergaer and around 3,000 mourners attended Muriel's funeral. She is buried at St David's Church, Penllergaer.

The case was featured in the 2020 BBC documentary *Dark Land: Hunting the Killers*, a true crime series about true crime, in which some of Wales' unsolved cold case murders are investigated by a team of experts, including the Chief Constable of Dyfed Powys Jackie Roberts, DCI Paul Bethell, former head of the South Wales Cold Case unit, geographic profiler Dr Sam Lundgren, forensic psychologist Prof Paul Britton and archive researcher Dr Nell Darby.

Bethell was able to discover the whereabouts of the gun used in the killing of Muriel Drinkwater, in the police force museum in Bridgend, sealed in a box with Muriel's name on it.

Forensics expert Dr Colin Dark was contacted, but unfortunately the gun had been handled so much over the years that it was impossible to extract any evidence from it.

Dr Lundgren said, 'with cold cases especially the sorts of cases we're looking at that go back to the 1940s it's a real challenge to see how new technology can help and potentially uncover new lines of enquiry.'

DCI Bethell stated that, 'reopening the case is as much about proving who didn't do it as much as who did, brutal murders such as Muriel's can have a terrible effect on a small village. There are people who have had to live with the finger of blame pointed at them for years and at last we have the scientific technology to say who it wasn't and also perhaps one day who it was.'

The case files showed that there had been a semen stain found on Muriel's coat. But the question remained, where was the coat? It was not until 2008 that it was found in a dark corner of a stockroom in a police station.

'I found the original clothing,' said Bethel. 'And we know even though it's been sixty years since it went into storage, that it was hers. Her name was written in copperplate: Muriel Joan Drinkwater.'

A circle marked the semen stain, now invisible to the naked eye, on the back of the coat.

Forensic experts were able to extract a partial DNA profile and due to improvements in technology, new evidence was now available.

Dr Dark is quoted in the documentary: 'We know 100 per cent that it is the killer's stain.'

This new evidence cleared Hubert Hoyles.

Hubert said: 'For years I lived with the knowledge that some people in the community suspected me, I could never hurt anyone or anything, but in a small close-knit community, people talk and I knew that in the eyes of some I was the murderer it blighted my life. Until now though I have not been able to prove beyond any doubt that I was not. This DNA finding has been a heck of a relief.

'I'd usually see Muriel as she made her way back from school and we'd exchange a hello,' recalls Hubert. 'I saw her that day she was just minutes from her house when we crossed on the path near the woods where she was killed. She must have been killed within a few moments of me seeing her and saying hello, she was a wonderful, lovely girl always singing, always so happy.'

The new DNA evidence also ruled out child killer Harold Jones.

Detective Chief Inspector Mark Lewis, the head of the South Wales Police's Specialist Crime Review Unit, said: 'The results of the forensic examination categorically confirm that Jones was not responsible for the murder of Muriel Drinkwater.

'Due to advances in forensic technology, we have been able to look again at evidence from the murder in 1946 and I am now able to rule out

Harold Jones completely as a suspect in this case. I have spoken to Muriel's family to bring them up to date with the latest details of this investigation.'

The crime had been dubbed as the 'Little Red Riding Hood murder', but just who was the big bad wolf?

The police have also been looking into whether there is a link between Muriel's murder and the unsolved murder of Sheila Martin in Dartford, Kent. Her body was found on 7 July 1946, a mere ten days after Muriel's brutally shocking attack. Sheila had been strangled with her own white hair ribbon.

After being last seen on a swing behind her house, a team of villagers undertook a search party, and the wood in which her body was discovered overlooked her home about half a mile away. She was found around fifty yards from the road.

There would have been thousands of people watching a motorcycle speedway that day at Brands Hatch about half a mile away from the crime scene. It's believed she was killed while the race was still in progress.

Although these crimes were hundreds of miles apart, could the horrific fate of these two young girls be linked or could there be two killers that have escaped their heinous crimes?

Another possible suspect mentioned in the documentary is Ronald Harries. He was involved in the Carmarthenshire farming community, although this community would lead to his undoing.

When that community spotted unmilked cows in a field in October 1953, they found this strange as the owner of the cattle, John Harries, was regarded as a very diligent farmer.

When it transpired that John and his wife Phoebe had not actually been seen for some time, the police launched an appeal asking for any information to their whereabouts. They had last been seen on Friday evening, 16 October 1953.

In the appeal, police described the couple as John having his own teeth with a few false on the bottom and Phoebe as having a very thin face with false teeth.

Interest was put upon a local man Ronald Lewis Harries (Ronnie), a farmhand from Pendine. Ronnie was a twenty-four-year-old loose relative of John Harries and his wife

Ronnie had told people that his uncle and aunt had gone off to London for a holiday and left him in charge at Derlwyn Farm. He went as far as telling the superintendent that he had taken the couple to Carmarthen Railway Station to get the train to London.

There were indeed two cases missing from their farm, which would back up Ronnie's version of events. But in reality, all was not what it seemed.

The locals who knew both John and Phoebe more closely stated that the couple had not actually been away on holiday for more than twenty years and that if in the highly unlikely event they had just packed up and headed for a break, London just would not be the obvious choice of destination for this quiet and reserved farming couple from Wales.

It was also suspicious that they had not even mentioned to any of their family or friends that they were even going on a trip.

The superintendent was convinced that he had the man responsible for the couple's disappearance, but he needed proof. He had nothing, no witness, no bodies, nothing but abandoned cattle and an empty farm.

Suspicion mounted when police learnt that a cheque made out to Ronald by his uncle had been altered from £9 to £909.

Ronnie lived at his parents' farm Cadno, an area too large to search for bodies manually, according to those around at the time. It is said that instead lengths of cotton were tied across the gaps and gateways in the hedges. They then proceeded to make Harries nervous. This seems to have worked as he went to check whether his burial site was still intact and in doing so he broke a thread. It is said that the broken thread led officers to the graves of John and Phoebe.

A kale field on Cadno Farm looked different to the others and the crops were not prospering, it was as if the area had been dug up recently. On 16 November 1953 the police found the concealed bodies of the couple hidden under the kale.

It has been suggested that they had both been summoned to the farm by Ronnie on Friday 16 October under the ruse that he wanted to show them a new well. John arrived first and was shortly thereafter hit on the head with a hammer and killed. Ronnie then went to collect Phoebe to take her to the same area where he had just viciously killed her husband in cold blood. He enticed her by saying that something had happened to John and that she should come quickly. Out of concern for her husband, Phoebe went along.

Sadly, Phoebe met the same fate as John, however following some tests that were carried out afterwards, it would seem that Phoebe had not died straightaway but was still alive when she had fallen to the ground.

Apparently on the way to his trial for murder, Ronnie was weirdly in a good mood, considering his current situation. He was talking jovially to the driver and even making plans for the future. He is quoted as telling a police officer, 'I'll buy you dinner in the Ivy Bush Hotel when this is over.'

The officer, who still lives in the area, has never had the promised dinner.

Crowds had gathered outside as Ronnie was escorted into the building. It is said that he sat quietly.

At the Carmarthen Assize in March 1954 Ronald Harries was charged with murder, but only one, even though there were two bodies, this being customary at the time. He was hanged at Swansea Prison, the last man to be sentenced to death at Carmarthen.

He had shown boldness in the lead up to the trial and defiance in the aftermath. But it is said that on the morning of his execution he was overcome with terror. People have suggested that this was out of fear and not out of any remorse.

At the time there was a suggestion that he had committed other murders, although nothing has ever been proven.

Dark Land: Hunting the Killers revealed that there is evidence that Harries was employed by the father of Muriel Drinkwater around the time of her death. DNA samples have been taken from Harries' relatives, but any results have not yet been made public.

Another revelation from the documentary revealed Muriel was carrying a satchel on that fatal day and there was a possibility that Muriel's killer could have removed something and kept it as a memento.

This thought comes after a children's book called *Little Playmates* turned up in a British Heart Foundation charity shop. Inside was an inscription that read 'From Aunty Moy and the girls to Muriel'. There was also a homemade bookmark bearing the name 'Muriel Drinkwater' and 'Easter 1944'.

When the customer who bought the book googled the name, he was horrified to find out about the murder and that he could be holding an item that could quite possibly have been so close to the horrific event.

Unfortunately, there is nothing on record to see who donated the book, but the documentary has put an appeal out asking if anyone has any information about this book to please contact the production team.

A veil of secrecy has now been thrown over the case of Muriel Drinkwater. The case files have been closed to the public and South Wales police have claimed that it has been done to improve the chances of finding the killer. Free availability of cold case files can interfere with investigation. As they also want to keep all information accurate, Sheila Martin's case files have also been closed.

The Welsh village has always known who its happy singing Red Riding Hood was, but still do not know who the big bad wolf was.

The main walk in this area that I have completed numerous times goes past where Muriel's family farm once stood. Park at Brynhyfryd Tircoed Forest Village, Swansea SA4 9JJ and then make your way through the gate near the top of the road that enters the forest. Then continue to do the short loop that heads back out to the village. This is a short walk and often quiet.

Although I have never walked here alone, it does have a slight spooky feel to it. You leave a modern housing estate with people going about their business and then are quickly surrounded by tall straight towering trees in vast rows with a path running through. Maybe its spooky feel comes from the fact that I know the history of the area and know who was walking there before.

For example, as you walk through the gate at Brynhyfryd to enter into the forest, hidden just to the side in the bushes is where Muriel's home would have once stood. Now only a few bricks remain scattered on the ground. Walking up Brynhyfryd Road around the area where Muriel's body would have been discovered, so close to her home, and then standing on the path next to where her family home was, was an incredibly moving experience because you can really appreciate how close this young girl was to arriving home.

Sadly murder stories are always going to be a part of history. I believe that names such as Muriel Drinkwater should never be forgotten for she was never allowed to grow up, instead remaining a twelve-year-old frozen in time and robbed of her bright future by an odious evil. I truly hope that although the killer could now quite possibly be dead, that his name does become known to bring some closure to the case and justice for Muriel, her family and community.

For those believing in ghosts, perhaps this area is haunted, but if you go down to these woods today don't expect a teddy bear's picnic.

Bricks that are believed to have been part of Muriel's family home.

Penllergaer Forest.

CHAPTER THREE

My Favourite Castles of South Wales

Cardiff Castle

Cardiff Castle sits within parkland in Cardiff, the capital city of Wales. It was one of the major strongholds of the South, a wartime defence for nearly 2,000 years.

In the first century AD, the Romans were the first people to build forts here. Made from timber, these fortifications would have provided a sanctuary to the legionaries who were stationed to protect part of the area between the Roman settlements Morodunum (Carmarthen) and Venta Silurum (Caerwent).

In 1066 at Hastings, William Duke of Normandy, later to be known as William the Conqueror, challenged Anglo-Saxon King Harold for the English throne. On Christmas Day, William would be crowned king, Harold having been defeated and killed. The Normans set about fortifying England with castles and when that was completed, their attentions soon turned to Wales.

William had to show his power and strength and so he built a castle at Cardiff.

There was just enough left of the fort built by the Romans to build upon. Even today if you stand facing the main entrance to the castle, on the left

My Favourite Castles of South Wales

This photograph shows part of Cardiff Castle.

adjoining side wall, you can see some red sandstone from the Romans amongst the rest of the wall.

In the eleventh century, the Normans constructed a motte-and-bailey castle. The term comes from French words *motte*, meaning mound, and *bailey*, meaning enclosure.

What we would now refer to as the keep can still be seen, however the original one would have been made of wood or stone. It would be used as a living space, but also as a prison for anyone who surrendered, allowing a type of house arrest to happen.

From this castle, a cousin and ally of William, Robert FitzHamon, ruled over Glamorgan.

Cardiff Castle became the power base from which the Normans would try to control Wales and its native inhabitants, all while policing the borders of England.

From the 1260s, Anglo-Normans and the Welsh were still fighting for control and FitzHamon's fortress was reinforced with stone by Gilbert de Clare who was responsible for the building of Caerphilly Castle.

Following William the Conqueror's death, his three sons all wanted the throne. The eldest, Robert, nicknamed Robert Curthose due to a joke about his height, was said to be weak and easily influenced. He had fallen out with his father more than once and at the time of William's death had been banished aboard. Hence the middle son, William Rufus, was crowned as William II.

In 1100 he was killed in a hunting accident by a stray arrow in his back and the youngest son, Henry, got his turn on the throne, as one of his brothers was dead and the other was fighting aboard in the Crusades.

Robert was unimpressed about losing the crown to not just one, but to two younger brothers. He began to raise troops to challenge Henry I. But this would only lead to Robert's undoing as in 1106 in a clash with Henry at Normandy, Robert was defeated and captured.

Henry wanted to do away with his brother for good and had him locked up indefinitely. It was in 1126 that Robert was brought to Cardiff Castle, after spending twenty years in the West Country. He was by this time in his seventies and in 1134 at eighty years old he died while still imprisoned at Cardiff Castle.

During his time at Cardiff, Robert spent some of his time learning the Welsh language and writing. In a translated line of one of his poems he wrote, 'Woe to him that is not old enough to die,' which is highly suggestive of his feelings about his confinement.

Cardiff Castle was about to enter an era of much blood and execution.

During the twelve and thirteenth centuries the castle's defences were constantly being beefed up. From the keep up on the hill to the southern gatehouse, a huge wall was built splitting the bailey into two.

In the early fourteenth century, Cardiff Castle passed into the hands of the Despenser family. It would be in this era that the castle would become a most feared symbol.

Hugh Despenser was a merciless and bloodthirsty character. He was a favourite of England's unpopular King Edward II. In 1307, he became Lord of Glamorgan. Despenser was despised in England due to his influence over the considered foolish king.

In 1316, a spout of bad weather and famine hit Wales. Llywelyn Bren, a Welsh lord, provoked by the hardships he was surrounded by, heroically led a revolt against the king, which soon spread through South Wales.

Edward II sent two thousand men into Wales to crush Bren, who headed for the Brecon Beacons hills. With the English now approaching in two directions, Bren surrendered in 1316.

Bren's conditions for his surrender were that he alone would be punished. This noble decision was regarded as extremely chivalrous by his captors, and they asked the king to pardon him. Despite this request coming from high-ranking lords, a pardon was not on the cards for Bren.

Two years after his capture, he was transported to Cardiff Castle and into the hands of one Hugh Despenser. This would spell disaster for Bren as Despenser, to send a stark message, wanted Bren dead.

There would be no fair trial, no justice, there was no interest in letting him go. Despenser saw this as his opportunity to let the lords who had spoken up against him know his strength and power. He sentenced Bren to being hanged, drawn and quartered. This was a terrible way to die, inflicting much pain and distress. Being dragged behind a horse, choked with a noose and disembowelled whilst still alive was one of the slowest and most agonisingly horrific deaths imaginable.

The death of Bren angered the Welsh and was likely to have been on the mind of Owain Glyndŵr when he stormed the castle in 1404 as part of his rebellion.

With a taste for blood, Despenser did not just terrorize Wales, but for the following four years he would become the power behind Edward II's throne.

However, eventually his evil deeds would come back to bite him. Despenser's influence had strained the relationship between the king and his wife Queen Isabella. While in self-imposed exile in France, she teamed up with Welsh baron Roger Mortimer and together they launched an invasion which saw them overthrow the king and the evil Despenser.

In a kind of poetic justice, Despenser was sentenced to the fate that he had inflicted upon Bren.

It's believed that whilst imprisoned Despenser attempted to starve himself in an attempt to escape his fate.

In a stained-glass window at the castle, Despenser's coat of arms is portrayed upside down to show his disgrace and shame. With his death, one of Cardiff Castle's most violent periods came to a close.

In the following centuries the castle would be tested to its limit by some of the bloodiest rebellions in British history.

In the fourteenth century, the castle symbolized the power of the English over the Welsh and so it would always be a target.

In the fifteenth century the last big Welsh rebellion began. In 1403, Owain Glyndŵr led a revolt against king Henry IV, burning the city of Cardiff and besieging the castle.

With the castle running extremely low on food, and with only twenty-four cannonballs left, it surrendered.

This was a stunning victory for the Welsh and although the English would reclaim Cardiff, it would take years to cool down Glyndŵr's rebellion.

In retribution the English passed penal laws that stripped the Welsh people of their rights, including no weapons, no holding public office and no speaking their own language. This was the English revenge after their humiliation. The Welsh were treated like second-class citizens.

Cardiff had become subdivided with people within the castle walls having different rights to people outside of the walls. Cardiff had become subdivided.

After the defeat of Glyndŵr, the castle was passed on to the Beauchamp family. They built new lodgings near the west wall.

In 1551, the young king Edward VI and his guardian William Herbert took possession of the castle and expanded it further.

In the seventeenth century in 1642, the English Civil War broke out and the castle was besieged several times.

It was first held by the Parliamentarians and then by the Royalists. The castle was badly damaged thanks to the use of gunpowder changing warfare.

From 1776 until 1947 the castle was owned by the Bute family, who definitely left their mark on not just the castle but Cardiff as a whole.

In 1766, Charlotte Jane Windsor married a wealthy Scottish landowner, John Stuart, first Marquess of Bute. During their time at the castle, the 1770s architect Henry Holland and landscaper Lancelot Capability Brown redesigned the castle gardens and accommodation.

More restorations took place during the 1820s under the second Marquess of Bute, who based himself at the castle during the events of the Merthyr Rising of 1831 and led the government response.

By the nineteenth century the super fuel was steam, coal mines and steelworks were in abundance.

In order to have steam, you needed coal.

The second Marquess of Bute understood the value of coal and exploited it, but someone had to dig it out of the ground. Transport was needed from the valleys to transport coal and iron around the world. He built Cardiff Docks for exports, making Cardiff one of the world's biggest ports, busier even than New York. There was a boom in the city's industry and population.

The third marquess John Crichton-Stuart inherited his father's estate after coming of age. A sixteen-year creative partnership began with architect William Burges, leading the castle to be transformed into a Gothic style medieval mansion.

Among the ornate rooms, the Arab Room in the Herbert Tower boasted an elaborate Moorish ceiling that was hand decorated in gold leaf, marbled walls and floors, cedar cabinets with silver and statuettes of eastern deities. In the fireplace, Bute memorialized the architect by putting Burges' initials along with his own and the date. It was considered among the most remarkable of Victorian interiors in Britain.

It was to become the last room Burges worked on before falling ill. After he passed in April 1881, Burges' assistant William Frame continued the work at Cardiff Castle.

With their wealth, the Butes transformed the castle into their family home. This included the wall of stone-sculpted animals that can still be seen today and is one of my favourite things amongst many at the castle. It would become famous for its opulence.

In 1939, Britain would declare war on Nazi Germany. Cardiff had seen fighting numerous times, but it would be called into battle one more time and its medieval defences would have to stand up to a twentieth century enemy.

The Nazis targeted Cardiff Docks. During the Blitz, around 33 000 houses of Cardiff were destroyed and almost 400 civilians were killed. The fatalities could have been higher had it not been for Cardiff Castle.

As its walls had taken the worst that the Middle Ages had thrown at them, it was realized that they then could probably withstand German bombs as well. The castle was close enough to the city for people to flee to, and the medieval ramparts had four gaps leading to a network of tunnels deep below the rubble to lead people to safety. These tunnels can still be explored today.

After the war, the fifth Marquess of Bute owned the castle, but with his family's money now drastically reduced, he sold off properties and gave the castle and its grounds to the people of Cardiff. Thus ended Cardiff Castle's relationship with the Bute family after 181 years, having gifted Cardiff a lasting legacy.

The castle's fighting has now ceased and in its era of peace it enjoys many visitors with an interest in history and castles, while the battles of Cardiff take place on the turf of the Principality Stadium to a sea of red and the roar of 'Hen Wlad Fy Nhadau'.

The castle remains as a stark symbol of not only Cardiff's history, but of its evolution.

Castell Coch

Referred to as a fairy-tale castle, at first glimpse, it's not hard to understand why. The castle's towers with their cone shaped rooves spark an image of Rapunzel and her tower.

Castell Coch stands within a beautiful scenic setting, rising out of the beech woods of Fforest Fawr. It is a stunning architectural masterpiece of the High Victorian era. It combines splendid Gothic fantasy with an almost timeless fairy tale, although there is much more, just underlying this masterpiece of nineteenth century construction.

Unfortunately, there is no documentary evidence about this castle's construction, nor whether it played a part in any territorial conflict.

After the Norman conquest, a considerable castle that would have been constructed out of earth and timber was built on a natural ledge of limestone at the mouth of the picturesque Taff Gorge.

The De Clare Lords of Glamorgan in the thirteenth century were aware of the strategical nature of this site. They developed a stone fortress over the site's earlier defences.

Although the castle's existence as a medieval stronghold was relatively short, it's assumed by the structural evidence that it was damaged and ruined militarily in the early fourteenth century. Most likely this happened during the Welsh Rebellions between 1314 and 1316.

The towers and walls were nearly completely destroyed. Beneath the castle ruins, the River Taff became flanked by canal, road and railway, thus allowing the rich mineral wealth of the upper valleys to build the growing seaport of Cardiff, the profits of which helped fund the third Marquess of Bute's relationship with architect William Burges. Together they would embark on creating an eccentric, fabulous, stunning masterpiece, rising above the remains of the medieval fortress at the site.

As an infant, John Patrick Crichton-Stuart, third Marquess of Bute, inherited the foremost landholding and property rights of mid-nineteenth century Britain. He would grow up to be an extraordinary figure of Victorian nobility. He had a great interest in languages and antiquarianism and preferred to lead a secluded life.

In the best-selling novel *Lothair*, written by Benjamin Disraeli, the third Marquess of Bute found fame as its hero. The Butes were well-known to Disraeli, a Tory statesman, who had a link with the family's estates at Glamorgan through his patron Wyndham Lewis. a lawyer, politician and industrialist.

Upon Lewis' death, his interest in an area situated below Castell Coch called the Green Meadow estate, passed to Mary Anne Lewis, his widow. Disraeli would marry Mary in 1839.

Disraeli was an outsider to the London establishment, much like the third marquess. These two men first met socially in 1867 in Edinburgh.

Bute gained social fame from being featured as the hero in *Lothair,* published in 1870. Despite disliking politics and finding London society unappealing, the novel portrays him as a wealthy nobleman who celebrated his coming of age at his estate, and grappled with his relationship with the Catholic Church.

It was on 8 December 1868, that the third Marquess of Bute was received into the Roman Catholic Church and would become an ardent supporter of the Catholic cause. This was a split from his family's traditions and also caused Cardiff to be aghast.

An eligible bachelor, Bute would marry the granddaughter of the Duke of Norfolk, a Catholic aristocrat, in 1872 in Kensington.

Disraeli was in attendance. If he did share in the mid-Victorian concern regarding the appeal of Catholicism to aristocrats, it did not stop him from being a wedding guest.

This marriage would be a dynastic success for both families with Bute's succession secured by children, four in total: Margaret, John, Ninian and Colum.

As well as his love for Catholicism, he was also a fervent Celt and his interest in Scottish history and antiquities led to him indulging in purchasing and preserving neglected monuments of importance, such as Rothesay Castle.

He offered support towards the Welsh language, which he studied, for the National Eisteddfod and Welsh history.

His love for building extended to his two remarkable castles in Glamorgan: Cardiff Castle and Castell Coch.

The man to indulge Bute's medieval dreams was architect William Burges.

Burges' family wealth enabled him to travel widely and frequently which helped him gain knowledge of medieval art, architecture, furniture, metalwork and jewellery. He wanted to introduce a new style with its basis in early French Gothic to Victorian architecture. The two men would meet in 1865 when Bute travelled to Oxford and Burges achieved wide-reaching recognition for his work at St Fin Barre's Cathedral in Cork. They were very different, coming from disparate backgrounds and having differing theological interests and temperaments. Bute was reclusive and serious, while Burges was ravishing and social. Though there were differences, there was also common ground between these two men. They were both antiquarians, travellers, collectors and aesthetes. On meeting, a relationship immediately formed.

After a year, Burges put together his report on enhancing Cardiff Castle. The work started there on Bute's coming of age in 1868. The vast project was a commission of a lifetime for Burges, allowing him to realize his inner frenetic genius.

When Cardiff's enhancements were already advanced, the idea to start reconstructing the smaller site of Castell Coch came to fruition, following an archaeological assessment in 1871. The report on Castell Coch was submitted on 27 December 1872 to Lord Bute.

Burges did not like perspective drawings, he thought of them as superficial. Instead, he built project folios for his clients. In an account of the ruins, Burges shows a desire to have an understanding of their military character. He had read the report of 1850, and made the recommendation to Bute that in regard to the ruins, one simply left them as they were, or restore them making it into a country residence, for use in summertime.

To leave them as they were, the only repairs needed would be to keep the walls together. Bute, however, was acutely aware of the possibilities, including the type of work carried out for Rothesay Castle's partial reconstruction.

With his medievalist heart and with the trend of gothic revival strong, Bute was drawn to the idea of a full rebuilding. This rebuilding would take place during from 1875 to 1891.

The delay in starting work after the report was due in part to the work already underway at Cardiff. Burges paid careful attention to details, leaving nothing to chance. Many of his precisely detailed drawings with careful measurements have survived.

As Castell Coch was intended to be a summer home, some of the domestic arrangements show informality; the idea of it being used as a retreat after perhaps events like picnic parties. But this fantasy of medievalism would need a sizeable kitchen, water closets, servant stairs, separate doors to ensure family privacy and a central heating system.

In a letter to his wife on 9 May 1876, Bute noted that he had been to Castell Coch with Burges and stated that he believed reconstruction would go quickly. Another letter of Bute's shows he required a full residence even if it was only for occasional use.

In comparing the 1872 report to the working drawings and the completion you can spot a few changes that would have been introduced during the construction. One of these was the way Bute and his family gained access to the banqueting hall. It appears that Burges' first intention was to have the entry point through the central doorway, that is now blocked, from a corridor in between the keep tower and the upper end of the hall block. However, in a drawing there is a revision showing a courtyard window being modified to provide an external doorway. It was a big redesign of the accommodation within the keep tower and the adjacent gatehouse to block the doorway at the eastern end of the hall. More changes shown were features that were removed from the planned silhouette, for example, a small watchtower with a crenellated parapet rising above the newel stair on the courtyard side of the Keep Tower.

Construction work on the main structure of the castle was completed by the end of 1879, including the late provision of central heating. Renovation of the interiors was just starting when Burges sadly died suddenly in April 1881. Only the banqueting hall decor and furnishings were almost complete by this date.

Luckily the craftsman who continued the work had access to Burges' incredible designs and most likely knew a lot of his intentions for the decor. By the time of Burges' sad passing, he had already made a creation that fulfilled Bute's wishes. The final completion of the interiors only came about in 1891 as despite a strong team of artists headed by J.S. Chapel and overseen by William Frame, there was perhaps a lack of momentum and coherence. However, the Burges spirit was not lost and the castle boasted brilliant designs throughout, such as Lady Bute's bedroom.

Castell Coch stands as one of the best Victorian triumphs of architectural composition. After the passing of Lord Bute, his daughter Anne retired to the castle after being widowed, until succession to the family estates and titles were completed. Lady Bute then received Castell Coch for life. The castle was used as a summer home on occasion and later became a reception point for hunts. It would remain as an exotic folly.

By the fifth Marquess of Bute in 1950, the castle was handed over to the Ministry of Works for conservation and protection. This castle is now in the care of Cadw (the historic environment service of the Welsh Government). There is no other house that William Burges designed that has so much of its original furniture. Following conservation work and with a 1901 inventory, practically all the major pieces have been identified and returned to their original rooms wherever possible. Replica fabrics have been added to help to portray the impression of how the castle would have looked on its completion in 1891.

One of my favourite sights at Castell Coch is the sculpture of the Three Fates of Greek mythology on the chimney piece in the drawing room. It was designed by Burges and carved by Thomas Nicholls. The conveyed message is that of human frailty: the fate Clotho oversees birth and spins the thread of life; the fate Lachesis measures it; and the fate Atropos cuts the thread at death. Underneath the fates are corbels showing the three ages of man. This is one of my favourite pieces as I have a keen interest in mythology and storytelling.

Another point of great interest for me is the Winch Room where you can see the working machinery needed for a drawbridge and portcullis. When I stood in this room, I experienced a real sense of power and authority as this room is able to stop unwelcome visitors. Even in the floor you can see the murder holes covered with wooden blocks. These are thought to have enabled residents of the castle to pour boiling water and oil on attackers.

Lastly, I should mention the main bedrooms.

Lord Bute's bedroom is spartanly decorated and furnished but is well lit due to windows on three sides. In this bedroom you can grasp Burges' intentions to give Lord Bute a true sense of controlling his defences. In the room is a stove-like fireplace with a circular flue. Carved around the cornice are foliage and small animals. There are a freestanding owl and cockerel that are carved on to either side of the chimney breast, symbolizing dusk and dawn.

Lady Bute's room's furnishings were not completed until 1891, but the concept was established by Burges prior to his death in both his drawings and a model. However, the decorative details were left for Campbell, Frame and Bute to agree on. There is a two-stage mirrored dome that rises under the hidden trusses supporting the iconic conical roof. There is an oriental feel to this dome, with painted panels reminiscent of the Aesthetic movement and which act as a contrast to the Gothic arcading.

Burges was passionate about Arabic and Moorish architecture from his travels in the 1850s to Sicily and Constantinople. You can see this influence at Cardiff Castle in the Arab Room of 1880-82. At Castell Coch, you can spot oriental influence in the subdued colours of the cavorting monkeys, on the ceiling above his wife's bed, of which Lord Bute disapproved.

Chepstow Castle

William the Conqueror, Duke of Normandy and King of England, was surrounded and supported by an inner circle of confidants that included his kinsfolk and members of leading families of his duchy.

According to writing from the eleventh century, William of Poitiers claimed the most highly considered of these confidants was William FitzOsbern, who William the Conqueror had known since they had been youths.

After the Battle of Hastings in 1066 and William was crowned king, he rewarded his loyal supporters. William FitzOsbern became the first Earl of Hereford and gained lands, including Chepstow.

English chronicler Orderic Vitalis recorded that William had sent FitzOsbern to battle the Welsh, although this was written some fifty years after the event. But it's clear that FitzOsbern was an extremely trusted

Chepstow Castle.

confidant as he was appointed as one of the vice-regents of England when William returned to Normandy in 1067.

FitzOsbern met his death at the Battle of Cassel in Flanders in 1071. His son Roger de Breteuil succeeded him. Considered to be weaker in character and having a dubious loyalty to King William, de Breteuil would even try to overthrow him in 1075 by plotting with Ralph, Earl of Norfolk and Suffolk.

The barons who were loyal to FitzOsbern's memory, captured de Breteuil by the River Severn. He was imprisoned and his estates were relinquished to the crown.

It states in the *Domesday Book*, completed in 1086, that it was FitzOsbern who built the castle at Chepstow, one of a number of fortifications built to help secure the border between England and Wales. The castle had natural as well as man-made defences due to the shape of the river cliffs it stands upon.

Roger de Breteuil had forfeited the estates of his father to the crown, including Chepstow Castle, and they would remain within royal hands through the reigns of William l, William ll and Henry l.

This photograph demonstrates some of Chepstow Castles natural defences.

In fact, the castle would remain within royal hands until around 1115 when Henry 1 granted lordship to a Walter fitz Richard de Clare, whose family would hold the castle for most of the twelfth century. Although they do not appear to have authorized any major work at Chepstow, Walter was responsible for the foundation of Tintern Abbey that was built near the castle in 1131.

Earl Richard, Walter's son and the conqueror of the Irish province of Leinster, died in 1176, leaving behind a son Gilbert and a young daughter Isabel as heirs to his estates. Isabel was a minor and therefore made a ward of Henry ll.

Isabel did spend some time at Chepstow, but the castle would be held by the crown on her behalf. She became a sought-after heiress and in 1189 was promised by the king in marriage to his loyal knight William Marshal.

He was the youngest son of an English knight and as such had little hope of inheriting any wealth or property. Whilst still a teen, he travelled to France and was admitted into the household of his kinsman, William de Tancarville, Chamberlain of Normandy.

It was here that William Marshal had the chance to gain experience of politics, country life and first-class military training.

At twenty, he was knighted. With only his armour and horses as possessions, he began to gain a reputation as a soldier. He was apparently handsome and confident and loyal, which attracted royal patrons, one of whom was Eleanor of England in 1168.

In frequently turbulent times, Marshal would come to act as a tutor and companion to the young Prince Henry. Marshal became successful enough to raise his own banner with its red lion rampant on a background of green and gold. Whilst Henry was dying in 1183, the loyal Marshal was given the responsibility of taking his cloak to the Church of the Holy Sepulchre in Jerusalem. On his return, he would join the military household of Henry II. Marshal would then constantly be in action defending the king's interests in France.

He was rewarded in 1187 with the grant of the royal estate of Cartmel in what was then Lancashire, now Cumbria.

Two years later, there would be a rebellion against the king by his own son Richard. Marshal's loyalty to the old king remained, but he would spare Richard in a skirmish when he could have taken his life. Richard was crowned king in 1189 and would honour his father's wish in recognition of Marshal's loyalty and gave him in marriage to heiress Isabel de Clare. From being a poor although brave knight, Marshal had transformed into one of the richest and most powerful men in the kingdom.

Throughout the reign of Richard I, Marshal would stay active in politics. He would go on to support King John's accession and was awarded the title of Earl of Pembroke in 1199 and was given many lands. And even though he lost the king's favour by 1250, Marshal acted as John's chief negotiator in the drafting of the Magna Carta. He then remained as the king's most important counsellor until John's passing. Marshal then acted as regent of England for the young King Henry III up until Marshal's death in 1219.

With his marriage to Isabel de Clare, he made many improvements to his wife's lands, including extensive additions to Pembroke and Chepstow Castles. He had newly acquired wealth, had a position of governance in the Kingdom of England, as well as a knowledge of advanced military techniques and this made him an ideal person to create a comfortable, but formidable fortress. On Marshal's death, he was succeeded by each of his five sons in turn and they held his estates until 1245.

When Marshal's first son, also William, passed away in 1231, his brother Richard succeeded him as Earl of Pembroke. He was to quarrel with Henry III, and after civil war almost broke out, Richard retreated to Ireland and was killed there in 1234. Henry had revisited Chepstow before the rift, and he had spent time at the castle in December 1232.

Gilbert succeeded Richard and reconciled with the king. Royal favour was shown with a grant of land in Cardigan and Carmarthen and the custody of Glamorgan. Gilbert's death in 1241 resulted from injuries sustained in a tournament held at Ware in Hereford. His brother Walter was next in line before both he and youngest brother Anselm died in 1245.

The Marshal brothers had not only extended Chepstow's western defences, but also transformed the great tower.

As there was no male heir in 1245, the estate was divided between William Marshal, first Earl of Pembroke's, five daughters and their descendants, with Chepstow Castle passing to the oldest sister Maud. She married Hugh Bigod, the third Earl of Norfolk and when Maud died their son Roger inherited Chepstow Castle. Roger passed away in 1270 and his nephew of the same name became the fifth Earl of Norfolk.

This was during the reign of Edward I. To start with, Roger was a loyal servant to the king, supporting him during the Welsh Wars of 1276 to 1277 and 1282 to 1283. This was when Edward battled against Llywelyn ap Gruffud of Gwynedd. Wales would eventually be subdued. Roger also acted as a peacemaker on Edward's behalf in Ireland in 1280; and he helped suppress a Welsh uprising in South Wales in 1287.

During this time, he built a stone wall around Chepstow to control access and taxes. His titles and lands brought him huge wealth, but he also inherited considerable debts to the crown from his father and uncle. It was these debts and the demands for tax to pay for the fighting in Wales, France and then Scotland that led to a dispute with the king. More tension between them came from Edward's usurpation of his rights as Earl Marshal. From 1293 to 1296, pressure mounted culminating in the king demanding an invasion of France and an expedition to Flanders.

At a parliament in Salisbury, Earl Roger refused his order to lead an army to Gascony instead of acting as Earl Marshal besides the king in Flanders. Following this it is said that he and Humphrey de Bohun, Earl of Hereford, raised a force of 1,500 cavalry and some foot soldiers and refused to join in the king's muster. They marched into the Exchequer and forbade officials from raising taxes for the war.

With a partnership with the City of London together they looked for confirmation from the Magna Carta and the Charter of the Forest and made the demand to include a clause that the king would obtain the consent of his subjects before the levy of a new tax. With the success of William Wallace at the Battle of Stirling Bridge in Scotland, the king's hand was forced. Edward I agreed to the earls' demands to make sure of their loyalty in the Scottish campaign.

Although he achieved what he set out to do, Roger's power appears to have collapsed. His ally Humphrey died in 1298 and according to Walter of Guisborough, Roger had found himself in financial trouble after spending his wealth raising an army against the king. In 1302 his titles and lands were temporarily relinquished to the king. He would regain them weeks later with the king giving him an extra £1,000 of farmlands' rent on the agreement that if he died without a direct heir the Bigod's state would then be reverted to the crown. Edward went on to pardon Bigod debts in 1305 and when he passed childless in 1306, his estates including the lordship and Chepstow Castle were given back to royal hands.

King Edward outlived Bigod by a mere seven months. The estates were then inherited by Edward II. He took interest in the castle and in 1312 he made his half-brother, Thomas of Brotherton, the Lord of Chepstow. Some repairs were made. Springalds were made good and the armoury was being replenished regularly during the constableship of the king's favourite Hugh Despenser the Younger, who would be granted the castle in 1324.

Instead of facing off against the rebel forces led by the king's now estranged wife, Isabella of France, and her lover Roger Mortimer, Edward II and Despenser fled to Chepstow Castle, which had been provisioned maybe in the expectation of a siege. Both men attempted to escape by sea to Ireland. However, they were forced to land at Cardiff and were eventually captured. Despenser was executed and the king met his death in Berkeley Castle.

In 1403, the castle at Chepstow was passed to Thomas Mowbray, Earl of Norfolk. He was ordered to defend and make provisions in the castle in case a man called Owain Glyndŵr came knocking. Glyndŵr's advance was stopped at Usk and the castle saw no action.

Chepstow again provided refuge to fallen royal favourites during the Wars of the Roses, 1455-85. When the Battle of Edgcote ended in Yorkist defeat in 1469, Richard Woodville, Earl Rivers and his son fled the Earl of Warwick, but were made prisoners at Chepstow and were eventually beheaded at Kenilworth on 12 August 1469.

Charles, first Earl of Worcester, was cousin to both Henry Tudor and Lady Margaret Beaufort.

Henry Tudor in 1485 landed at Milford Haven in Pembrokeshire. After the success of the Battle of Bosworth, Charles' career was to prosper under his new king. In 1496, Charles became a Knight of the Garter and occupied offices in the king's household. He married Elizabeth, daughter of William Herbert, Earl of Huntington. Through this marriage, he acquired the lordships of Gower, Kilvey, Tretower, Crickhowell, and Raglan, and in 1504 became Baron of Herbert. On the death of Elizabeth's uncle, Sir Walter, in 1507, he became Lord of Chepstow. Therefore, he had become the most powerful man in South Wales. He was influential in Henry VIII's succession and was made Lord Chamberlain, head of the royal household.

His shining hour came when he was placed in charge of the negotiation of the truce between England and France. This resulted in a remarkable meeting of Henry VIII and the French King Francois I, along with their entourages just outside Calais at the Field of Cloth of Gold in June 1520.

When Charles died, he was buried at St George's Chapel in Windsor Castle as a reward for his service. Charles made substantial changes to the castle at Chepstow, the first to do so since Roger Bigod. He changed the lower bailey into a court by modifying its surrounding buildings. He relocated his private apartments to a complex of buildings on either side of the middle bailey.

A civil war broke out in 1642. Chepstow Castle belonged to Henry Somerset, the fifth Earl and later first Marquess of Worcester, who was a devoted Roman Catholic and vowed his devotion for King Charles I. The castle was in a very strategic location due to it being at the entrance to South Wales. From it you could control the Severn Estuary which had links to Bristol, an important royalist stronghold. In 1643 there was an advancement into Monmouthshire by the Parliamentarian general Sir William Walter, but he did not take Chepstow Castle and he was forced to withdraw.

It was after the fall of Bristol in 1645, when King Charles I's cause was becoming hopeless that the Parliamentarians would force the surrender of Chepstow. Thomas Morgan, in charge of the parliamentary forces, set up a battery of three guns on the hill overlooking the castle with a force of over 900 men. Edmund FitzMorris along with his 110 men were made to surrender. Along with the capture of an important castle, there were eighteen cannon, barrels of gunpowder and a vast store of provisions.

After King Charles was defeated and captured in 1648, some extreme royalists led uprisings resulting in a second phase of fighting. The main man was Oliver Cromwell, who whilst en route to reduce Pembroke, attacked the town of Chepstow with its walls lined with royalists and their muskets. Nicholas Kemeys, the castle governor, retreated into the castle with his 150 men. Cromwell demanded surrender; however, this was refused and Cromwell left Colonel Ewer and his men and four cannon to reduce it. They managed to destroy the garrison's guns and hit the interior with mortar shells. With Ewer's men prepared to storm the castle, the garrison surrendered and as a result Kemeys was shot.

The lands of the Marquess of Worcester were declared as forfeit after the Civil War and Chepstow Castle was given to Cromwell. Parliament spent £300 on repairs of the castle in 1650 and it was changed into a military barracks and became a prison for political dissidents. However when Charles II was restored to the throne in 1660 the town and the Lordship of Chepstow was returned to the Marquess of Worcester. But the king retained the castle as a barracks and fort. The eldest son Henry, Lord Herbert was appointed as its governor. He had to keep the fortification in good repair and was charged with raising a company of 100 men. Although Henry would succeed to his father's titles in 1667, he did not live at Chepstow Castle. His main residence was Badminton House.

Chepstow Castle also acted as a prison for those who were thought to have been a threat to King Charles II. Colonel Robert Overton, a parliamentary commander and politician, was brought to the castle in 1661. Although he was free again by 1663, he would be rearrested and taken to Jersey.

Another prisoner here was Henry Marten, a republican politician and one of the fifty-nine people to sign King Charles I's death warrant. He escaped execution on the restoration of Charles II, unlike many of his fellow regicides, but was sentenced to life imprisonment. He spent time at Lindisfarne Castle, the Tower of London, Windsor Castle and in 1668 he was moved to Chepstow where he was held in what is now known as Marten's Tower. Along with his mistress, he occupied the first-floor room with his servants in the one above. He was allowed guests and was able to communicate with the local gentry. Marten is buried at Chepstow parish church.

The end of the castle was approaching by the 1680s. The Duchess of Beaufort wrote to her husband, 'I do most humbly beseech you never to think of more building at Chepstow'. She said she'd rather it came down and that she preferred her new mansion at Badminton, Gloucester.

In 1685, the garrison was abandoned and parts of the castle, such as the upper parts of the great tower and internal fittings, were removed and demolished. The lower bailey was repurposed for industrial use during the late eighteenth century. Many visitors took tours down the River Wye from Ross through Monmouth and Tintin to Chepstow, stopping at the castle, where the Williams family served as custodians. A bell at the main gate would summon them when visitors arrived. In the nineteenth century, the industrial works were removed, and the eighth Duke of Beaufort cleared the castle's interior, planted trees, and constructed rustic seating areas.

By the late nineteenth century, conversion was started by the Beaufort estate and continued by the Lysaght family, who came to acquire the castle in 1905, using the local architect Eric Francis. Interest was growing locally as the castle became the venue for yearly medieval pageants and in 1913 was featured in the film *Ivanhoe*. By 1953, the Lysaght family placed the castle under the guardianship of the state and it is now maintained by Cadw.

Caerphilly Castle

Caerphilly Castle impressively stands as a great fortress surrounded by water. I remember my very first glimpse of this magnificent castle and how it evoked a feeling of Aladdin and his magic carpet as it appeared to be floating effortlessly on the water.

This photograph depicts the front side of Caerphilly Castle, taken from a nearby path.

The castle is not situated in a classic defensive location; instead, it sits on the floor of a natural basin, situated in scenic rolling hills. This adds to the picturesque and tranquil scene you are greeted with when you visit the castle. Don't be fooled by the peacefulness; this castle has seen its fair share of excitement, having been embroiled with very powerful men and, interestingly, also some strong women.

The strength of Caerphilly comes from its carefully planned sequence of wall, gatehouses and towers, with the added protection of being surrounded by moats and lakes. Together the architecture and near impregnable water defences made Caerphilly one of the most formidable castles of the British Isles. The castle, of course, was intended to elicit an aura of power, prestige and a right of lordship, even to be held by force if necessary.

This castle is one of the best architectural achievements of the Middle Ages. It was built by Gilbert de Clare, Earl of Gloucester, Hereford and Marcher Lord of Glamorgan. He was easily the richest baron in the country and his power unmatched by contemporary Marcher lords.

The Lordship of Glamorgan had passed to the De Clare family in 1217. The founder of the family, Richard, had been part of the Norman invasion of 1066 and had thus been rewarded. He was given estates in Tonbridge, Kent and Clare, from where the family took their new name, in Suffolk.

The De Clare's were set to become the most powerful baronial family in thirteenth century England. They had been Earls of Herefordshire since the 1140s, but now with the acquisition of the lordships of Glamorgan and neighbouring Gwynllwg, they became very powerful.

When Richard de Clare died in 1262, his son Gilbert, who was not quite nineteen yet, was most likely expected to inherit Richard's vast estate, although the king at the time appeared determined to keep these under his royal control – perhaps in part due to the increasing threat that was posed to the Welsh Marcher lordships by Prince Llywelyn ap Gruffudd of Gwyneth.

The king stood firm in his decision which angered the young Earl Gilbert, whose nickname was 'The Red', partly due to the colour of his hair, but also due to his fiery temperament.

Gilbert refused to pay homage to the king's son in 1263, instead aligning himself with Simon de Montfort, Earl of Leicester. On returning to England, Simon was determined to revive baronial pressure for reform, and even though the king released Gilbert's inheritance just a few months later to secure his allegiance, their differences were not completely resolved.

With the outbreak of the Civil War in 1264, Gilbert, along with De Montfort, went to Lewes in Sussex. During a battle, the Royalist force along with King Henry and Lord Edward were compelled to surrender and negotiate. King Henry had to face the fact that his rule going forward would be supervised by a council of nine. These men were all appointed by De Montfort.

Gilbert quickly grew tired of De Montfort's autocratic rule and of the grand patronage that was bestowed upon his family and his foreign knights. By May 1265, things were further exasperated when Gilbert's brother Thomas helped Lord Edward escape from detention.

Edward was then met by Gilbert at Ludlow. In attendance was another powerful Marcher lord, Roger Mortimer.

As a thank you for their support, the prince agreed to rule through native Englishmen and restore the old Lords of the Kingdom. But in De Montfort's eyes, this was an act of treachery and he tried to negotiate an agreement with Llywelyn ap Gruffudd to proclaim De Clare as a rebel.

If the forces of Llywelyn could be brought into play here, it could damage De Clare's interests in South Wales.

With time now of the essence, Gilbert, Edward and Mortimer joined forces. Their move was to attack De Montfort at his key stronghold in Kenilworth. De Montfort escaped, but just a few days later on 4 August 1265, he was forced to engage against the Royalist army at the Battle of Evesham. He was brutally murdered and dismembered on the battlefield.

Now all the Royalists had to do was squash the remaining De Montfort supporters, especially those at Kenilworth under Simon's son. This involved an extended siege that lasted from Easter to Christmas, probably due to the castle's defences of massive stone and water.

The end of the siege should have concluded the conflict once and for all, however there was still not complete peace between De Clare and Henry III.

Gilbert's role had been vital to royal success, though he received little in way of reward. He was still hostile towards the king's government, particularly with regards to the treatment of rebels or the Disinherited as they came to be known.

Gilbert marched on London suddenly, prompting a popular rising in the city.

The two sides were able to agree on peace terms and thus ended the Civil War at last.

As this was all playing out in England, there had been transformation of the political and military situation in Wales. This was due to the rise to power of Prince Llywelyn ap Gruffudd.

Llywelyn along with his brother Owain had had success in the Kingdom of Gwyneth in 1246. During the previous six years, they had witnessed their uncle Dafydd be undermined and humiliated by Henry III and thus struggle dynastically.

What had been achieved by Dafydd's father, Llywelyn ab Iorwerth, had been lost to the king.

In secret, Llywelyn made valuable alliances with his fellow Welsh Lords. In 1255 after he had defeated his brothers, he became the sole ruler of Gwynedd and along with his allies expanded territorial control over the next three years.

In 1258 the Magnates of Wales gave Llywelyn their allegiance and as a result he became Prince of Wales.

In the same year, Henry III was forced into agreeing to a truce with Llywelyn, having been embroiled with the baronial unrest in England. This however was broken in 1262, with Llywelyn continuing to exploit political disarray happening in England. As a result, Llywelyn continued to expand his territorial supremacy.

It benefitted Llywelyn to side with the De Montfort faction and campaign against the Marcher lords that were loyal to the king.

In 1265, Llywelyn entered a formal alliance with De Montfort with his title as Prince of Wales being officially acknowledged. But this abruptly ended when Earl Simon was killed on the field of Evesham. The political uncertainty continued in England, and it was assumed a Royalist offensive against Wales was out of the question.

Henry III through the Treaty of Montgomery, sealed in September 1267, was finally obliged to make peace with Llywelyn ap Gruffudd.

Llywelyn's claim to the title Prince of Wales was now accepted by Henry, including recognising that he and his successors should hold the principality by hereditary right. He was also allowed to keep much of what he had conquered and was guaranteed the homage of the Marcher lords of Wales.

The Marcher lords were not happy with Llywelyn's confirmed status and new powers.

Gilbert felt once again that there were questions raised around the loyalty of the Welsh rulers in the north and Glamorgan. He had already gone on to the offensive in January 1267 when he had moved into the upland Senghenydd, imprisoning in Ireland its ruler Gruffudd ap Rhys.

On 11 April 1268 Gilbert began building Caerphilly Castle, primarily to secure his newly annexed territory in northern Senghenydd and to oversee access from Cardiff.

It would be an overt symbol of Gilbert's authority, thus incensing Prince Llywelyn.

There is no certainty of whether open warfare happened before the castle's construction, or as a reaction to it, but a battle did brutally take place that year. A truce was agreed thanks to the efforts of the king, although this was a dispute that was destined to continue.

Without any signs of a permanent solution two years on, Llywelyn lost his patience altogether in October 1270. He attacked the rising fortress at Caerphilly. Gilbert in response launched reprisals and was able to secure the surrounding upland defences.

Once again King Henry III was obliged to intervene. He appointed two bishops to take control at Caerphilly and both sides agreed to a truce until a traditional hearing could be held the next July.

But De Clare's constable at nearby Cardiff Castle managed to trick his way into the Caerphilly fortress with forty armed men and was able to quickly overpower and eject the bishops' small garrison.

It was undoubtedly clear that Gilbert was absolutely determined to win this struggle. He remained loyal to the crown despite his troubled relationship with the royal family.

Whilst Henry was dying at Westminster in 1272, Gilbert was summoned to his bedside where he promised to keep the peace and protect the kingdom until Lord Edward returned from the Crusades.

Edward landed back in England in August 1274 as King Edward I and was greeted by Gilbert, Earl of Gloucester and John, Earl of Warenne. De Clare attended the king's coronation with 100 knights.

Prince Llywelyn, however, felt duped. His disputes with De Clare and Humphrey de Bohun showed that the Treaty of Montgomery did not provide any guarantees. If they were able to chip away at Llywelyn's authority on the borders, he would never have the territorial security that he craved.

With any chance of compromise rapidly disappearing, he felt the need to act. He wrote to King Edward, stating 'the rights of our principality are separate from the rights of your kingdom'. He pressed for restitution in the southern March.

In February 1274 he asked that De Clare and De Bohun be compelled to restore lands that he felt had been unjustly occupied and attained.

But rapidly other issues became apparent, such as Llywelyn's vision of an independent principality which was unmatched by the king's determination to assert his authority over Wales.

During 1276, Edward declared and labelled Llywelyn a rebel and invasion was now on the cards.

In the royal campaign of 1277, Gilbert de Clare's considerable private army proved to be vital, even though his relationship with Edward remained uneasy.

After the surrender of Llywelyn, De Clare was thanked for his expenses and labours.

In the king's second war against Llywelyn, Gilbert became head of the Royal Army in South Wales. Llywelyn was in a desperate situation. Even the Archbishop of Canterbury looked to start negotiations between the two sides, however the Welsh prince stated his people would rather die than pay homage to a stranger whose manners, laws and language were ignorant.

But in Edward's view, Llywelyn was a traitor, and the king now sought the total conquest of Wales.

In December 1282, Llywelyn was killed near Builth in mid Wales.

The triangle was in effect broken, the relationship between three men who had overseen the royal Marcher and Welsh interests over twenty years was now concluded.

Therefore, it's clear Caerphilly Castle was established during a very turbulent time, as I suppose many castles are if you think of what these fortifications represent.

De Clare had wanted a formidable fortress built; you could say that he succeeded in doing so.

The site chosen for the castle was drained of two streams: the Nant Y Gledyr and Nant Y Risca.

There probably would have been some knowledge of the Roman fort and of the Roman roads that ran south to Cardiff and north to Gelligaer and Brecon as they were most likely still in use.

In the completion of the first major phase of work in the mid-1270s, Caerphilly Castle stood primarily as a formidable fortress. There was a great hall, a chapel chamber and service routes built against the southern wall with seven comfortable rooms in two main gatehouses.

It was intended that the castle house a military garrison.

The main elements of Caerphilly Castle stand on a low ridge of glacial gravel.

The basic yet brilliant defences of the central and western islands were made by digging two large north-south ditches across the ridge and mounting up the soil.

On the east side of the central island, a platform acted like a dam to house the Nant Y Gledyr, making a big southern lake along with moats filled with water to the west, north and east of the inner ward.

Each of the new islands were contained by walls of stone which archers could mount as a first line of defence.

Even the corners ensured the widest possible field of fire with their sweeping curves.

The castle was also revolutionary in its design due to the number, size and sophistication of its gatehouses. As a unit, they controlled the access to the castle.

This idea of using concentric defences can also be noted at the Tower of London by Henry III's military engineers. Some have suggested that Gilbert may have used people from the office of the royal works to help design his castle.

The castle's defences have been tested on more than one occasion.

As previously mentioned, one of those being by Llywelyn ap Gruffudd, while another would be the uprising of Morgan ap Maredudd.

Morgan's forces managed to destroy much of the town, but the castle appears to have stood its ground.

While Caerphilly Castle was intended to house a military garrison under the command of a keeper or constable, there also had to be adequate accommodation for knights and their earl, and any distinguished guests.

However, in the final quarter of the thirteenth century, Caerphilly Castle saw both substantial additions and alterations which suggested that De Clare planned to make this his principal residence in South Wales.

My Favourite Castles of South Wales

A gatehouse at Caerphilly Caslte.

The castle was set to become a great country house for the Earls of Gloucester, all the while still in keeping with its original military intention.

It has been suggested that the building's design was conceptualized once the threat of war had abated. This new emphasis at Caerphilly can be compared, with the work that was undertaken at Chepstow Castle by the Earl of Norfolk and others at Pembroke.

These nobles and earls did not rely on permission from the king to wage wars, collect taxes, hold court or indeed build castles. It's as if they were able to act as independent princes, under the condition that they remained loyal to Edward and his policies.

After Caerphilly's transformation from a fortress into a country residence, the De Clares were responsible for one last phase of building at the castle which focused on the outer main gatehouse, along with its protecting hexagonal barbican, the northern dam platform with its wall and towers and the northern gatehouse. There was also the creation of another substantial lake around the north side of the castle.

Caerphilly Castle stood as an expressive example of the De Clare family's power, wealth and, let's face it, huge confidence.

The first time I laid my eyes on this castle, I thought to myself, this is not a place you would want to mess with, even today.

After the death of Earl Gilbert de Clare the Younger at the Battle of Bannockburn in 1314, there was a political vacuum in the southern March. Due to there being no male heir, King Edward II took the De Clare inheritance into his own care. But a period of violent unrest followed as custody of Glamorgan was granted to a sequence of tactless royal administrators.

There were even petitions to the authorities by the Welsh upland community. In Senghenydd, a member of the old Welsh aristocracy was particularly mistreated. Llywelyn Bren was a well-read, sophisticated man who had been entrusted with local offices during the time of young Gilbert, and he is described as a great and powerful man. He was most likely the son of Gruffudd ap Rhys, who was the last Welsh Lord of Senghenydd, deposed in 1267.

July 1315 saw Payne de Turberville, Lord of Coity be appointed as the king's keeper of Glamorgan. The same year saw the harvest fail which ultimately resulted in famine. De Turberville was ruthless in his attempt to extract as much revenue from the lordship as possible, but misjudged the

My Favourite Castles of South Wales

Looking up at the portcullis of Caerphilly Castle.

situation, angering the likes of Llywelyn Bren by removing them from their positions of responsibility.

The last straw proved to be when Llywelyn Bren was ordered to come before the king at parliament in Lincoln on 27 January 1316 having been accused of sedition.

The very next day, Llywelyn Bren launched his attack on Caerphilly, signalling a widespread revolt.

William de Berkerolles, the castle's keeper. was taken by complete surprise and was captured while he presided over a Court of Justice outside the castle walls. A number of his officers were also captured, and thirteen men were killed. Llywelyn quickly laid siege to the castle.

As quick as the revolt spread across Glamorgan, so did its devastation. Towns such as Neath and Kenfig were burnt; around ninety houses were destroyed at Llantrisant and its castle was captured with all defenders except the constable killed; and farms and mills were destroyed and devastated in the countryside. Caerphilly Castle did not escape damage as the outer ward was burnt down, the drawbridge was destroyed, and roofs were damaged.

However, a small garrison inside the castle held strong for six weeks, under the leadership of Gilbert's widow and heiress, Eleanor de Clare.

Under the command of William de Montague in early March, 150 men at arms and 2,000 footmen formed a Royal Army and assembled at Cardiff. They made their advancements north to provide relief. They encountered Llywelyn's army entrenched at the summit of Caerphilly Mountain.

The English inflicted the Welsh with heavy losses as they were able to outflank them, resulting in the relief of Caerphilly Castle. The garrison was stocked and the damage it had suffered was repaired.

The revolt came to an end on 18 March.

Payne de Turberville was removed from his office, his time as keeper of the lordship had been disastrous, and even with an inquiry that revealed injustices had happened, the rebels were still harshly treated.

Many of the community were fined and allowed to return to their lands, however 200 of the closest allies of Llywelyn Bren were required to pay heavy ransoms or subjected to long imprisonments.

Along with his wife and sons, Llywelyn Bren was taken to the Tower of London, but two years later Hugh Despenser, a new Lord of Glamorgan, had him brought to Cardiff and executed in the most brutal way. This act of cruelty contributed to the growing hatred for Despenser in the south of Wales.

The final De Clare earl, Gilbert, was only four years old when his father passed away; he had royal connections through his mother, Countess Joan, who was the daughter of King Edward I and the elder sister of King Edward II. Gilbert was brought up in the court of Edward I's second wife Margaret and two of his sisters were married to men who had significant influence on the life of young Edward II. Eleanor de Clare had married Hugh Despenser the Younger in 1306, while the next year Gilbert's other sister Margaret married Piers Gaveston.

It can be argued that possibly the early part of Edward II's reign was spoilt due to his devotion to Gaveston and the later part ruined by his strong emotional relationship with Despenser.

Gilbert de Clare supported the king loyally during a time that saw mounting baronial opposition to Gaveston. Gilbert attempted to mediate with the leader of the opponents, Thomas, Earl of Lancaster.

In 1314, the king was robbed of his powerful ally when Gilbert died at Bannockburn. The king soon found a second infatuation in Despenser the Younger whose father was a diplomat and had acted as a political adviser, as well as a mentor to Edward after he had been created Prince of Wales in 1301. The influence grew stronger once Edward became king.

It would be the introduction of Despenser the Younger into the Royal Court that would see a change in the fate of the nation forever. Through his wife Eleanor, he had obtained a third of the De Clare estates in 1317, including the Lordship of Glamorgan. He was made Chamberlain of the King's Household the next year. This gave him the power to control the royal finances and granted him access to the king's ear.

He even wanted to obtain more of the De Clare inheritance from his brothers-in-law, however after becoming so angered by his actions in 1321, a coalition of Marcher lords, including his brothers-in-law, rose up against him. They burned and destroyed his property; Caerphilly Castle was captured, its armoury raided and its records and charters taken to be destroyed.

To avoid any opposition, the king was obliged to exile both the elder and younger Despensers, however this would be short lived. The king gathered his loyal forces and welcomed back the exiled Despensers and eradicated any opposition during the Battle of Boroughbridge in Yorkshire in March 1322. The Despensers then enjoyed an unprecedented influence for the following four years in the running of the kingdom and were able to accumulate vast fortunes.

With this newfound wealth and power, Despenser remodelled Caerphilly Castle's great hall from June 1325 to the early part of 1326. He used the finest master craftsmen and along with money from his Italian bankers, he brought the great hall up to date with an ornately decorated style. The room was comfortable enough to entertain a king.

Despenser would come back down to ground with a bang, thanks to a woman – Isabella of France, Edward II's estranged wife, as she would overthrow the tyranny.

Isabella had refused since 1325 to return to England from a visit to France with Edward's son unless the Despensers were removed from court. In September 1326, taking matters into her own hands, she landed on the Suffolk coast with a small force and made her way to London unopposed.

With the castles of Bristol and Caerphilly already provisioned the king, with Despenser in tow, flew west with as much of the king's treasury as they could manage. By October, they arrived in Wales via Gloucester after lodging at Tintern Abbey. Then they moved on to Chepstow Castle before sailing into the port at Cardiff on 27 October and heading for the newly restored castle at Caerphilly. They stayed within the castle walls until 2 November.

Perhaps they expected to make a last stand here, however with no local support and with Isabella and her lover Roger Mortimer closing in, the king and Despenser had no choice but to flee once again. They headed to Margam and then to Neath before they were captured on 16 November near Llantrisant.

Despenser was executed on 20 November and King Edward was imprisoned. After ten months, he too suffered a brutal death at the hands of Mortimer. While this unfolded, the castle at Caerphilly was still besieged by the forces of Queen Isabella.

The council had been defiant under the control of John de Felton, Despenser's young son and a garrison of around 137 men.

William Lord Zouche was sent by the queen to take command of the besieging force in mid-February 1327 and by March, a surrender was agreed with the queen. Free pardons were given to all members of the garrison, including Despenser's heir.

An inventory was taken of the castle contents revealing a great number of valuables, provisions and weaponry that had been sent there by Despenser and the king. These included the king's ornate armour, silver vessels and plenty of food and drink to withstand a siege. The valuables were taken to Cardiff in six wagons, from there they were put on a ship to Bristol and finally made it back to London to be put under the care of the king's treasurer.

The pair had also taken valuables with them during their escape to Neath, but most were spirited away. A commission held in 1336 revealed that property to the value of £60,000 had been lost from the royal coffers.

After Hugh Despenser the Younger died in 1326, no major building took place at Caerphilly Castle. After its surrender in 1327, it was briefly in the hands of Queen Isabella, but in 1328 it was restored to Despenser's widow, Eleanor, and so the castle was once again held by a De Clare.

In 1329 William Lord Zouche abducted Eleanor and the couple married in secret without royal consent and then laid siege to the fortress at Caerphilly in a claim to the lordship. They were arrested by Roger Mortimer's men and ordered to pay a great fine of £50,000. The following year saw Mortimer's downfall and the lordship and castle of Glamorgan were restored to Eleanor once again, but this time along with her new husband William.

During the rest of the fourteenth century, Caerphilly Castle passed to descendants of Hugh Despenser and Eleanor de Clare. This saw several periods of royal custody until heirs came of age.

During the Welsh uprising of 1403 under Owain Glyndŵr, the English King Henry IV ordered the castle at Caerphilly to be garrisoned with armour, artillerymen and anything else that would be useful to hold back the Welsh.

Other castles in Glamorgan were besieged and sacked at the time, however there is not enough evidence showing that Caerphilly saw any major action during this time.

Caerphilly continued to be held by successive Lords of Glamorgan during the fifteenth and sixteenth centuries. By the time of Richard Beauchamp, Earl of Warwick, there appears to be a shift where Cardiff was restored as the main castle of Glamorgan. Significant additions were made there by Beauchamp, including a new residential range.

Caerphilly Castle was not completely overlooked as there was a conversion of the outer gatehouse into a prison for felons convicted at the local courthouse, and repairs were done to Felton's Tower and its sluice gates.

By the sixteenth century it seems interest was lost in the castle by its owners, and it was sadly allowed to fall into serious decay.

In around 1539 when antiquary John Leland visited the castle, he described it as 'Ruinus waulles of a wonderful thinknes, with just a single toure kept up for prisoners'.

The decay sped up from 1593 due to Henry Herbert, Earl of Pembroke leasing the castle to Thomas Lewis who took stones from Caerphilly to build his new Elizabethan mansion Y Fan.

Sadly there are no surviving records of the role of Caerphilly during the Civil War of 1640, though towards the north and east of the castle there is an earthwork that can be dated to the same period, most likely built by the castle's owner Philip Herbert, fourth Earl of Pembroke and loyal supporter of King Charles I. The masonry castle was not suitable to defend

Caerphilly Castle.

against repeated cannon fire and this compacted earthwork could act as a replacement, maybe whilst the Civil War was in progress or more likely in the aftermath.

A lot of the castle at Caerphilly was deliberately destroyed: the four corner towers of the inner ward and the main front of the inner ward appeared to have been blown up or undermined. This could have contributed to the astonishing form of the southern east tower or, as it's called today, the leaning tower of Caerphilly. If I'm being totally honest, this tower was my biggest reason for visiting the castle.

By the time of the reign of Victoria, any visitors to the castle would have found it in ruin.

The castle by this point was part of the largest estate in South Wales, owned by the Stuart family of Bute. The first Marquess of Bute John Stuart appears to have had an interest in the ruins and he tried to protect them.

The third Marquess of Bute, John's great grandson, was obsessed with the Middle Ages along with his equally fascinated architect William Burges.

The leaning tower or Caerphilly.

From 1868, Bute had begun his restoration and redecoration of Cardiff Castle, before turning his attention to Castle Coch in 1875.

With regards to Caerphilly, Bute's main contribution was to reroof the great hall so that he could provide lunch during a visit by the Royal Archaeological Institute in 1871. The windows and doorways were left as gaping holes.

It is worth noting that Bute did commission an accurate measured survey of the ruins from architect William Frame.

Some of the reconstruction drawings that feature in the survey suggest that the third marquess was thinking of a full-scale restoration, but it would be the fourth Marquess of Bute, John Crichton-Stuart who took on the challenge.

In contrast to his father's fascination with the medieval era, the fourth marquess seems to have been mainly driven by a sense of social justice.

Starting in 1928 with funds coming entirely from his own estate, he offered a programme of public works, with the aim to support the economy of the town of Caerphilly after the 1926 general strike and during the Great Depression.

With the start of the Second World War in 1939, any building work at the castle was brought to a halt. Some of the men working on the castle joined up, while the remaining older workforce was paid off. You can see in the rear face of the inner west gatehouse, where restoration was nearly completed apart from the replacement of two windows.

The significant parts of the restoration had been the northwest tower, the outer main gatehouse and bridge, the inner east gatehouse, the south dam and the southwest tower.

As leases of local business came up for renewal, they would be bought out and demolished, as it was the marquess' plan to clear buildings that obscured the ruins. He also did this with houses. The clearance enabled the construction of the great earthen bank and for the adjacent moat to be reflooded.

Not everyone appreciated these efforts. The Office of Works, which looked after many of Wales' ruined buildings, was uneasy. Their philosophy leaned more towards 'keep as found'.

In 1947, the marquess passed away and the estate was forced to sell properties in South Wales. By 1950 Caerphilly Castle was taken into state care and the Ministry of Works faced a dilemma as they were now responsible for a largely restored medieval castle, whose conservation had gone against their own philosophy, and which they had actively opposed.

Restoration would continue over the next sixty years or so including the repair of the two dams and the reflooding of the north and south lakes.

Since 1984 the castle has been under the care of Cadw and they have continued work, including reflooring the inner east gatehouse and southwest tower enabling visitors to explore the interior for the first time.

Pembroke Castle

One of the largest castles in Wales, Pembroke Castle is an impressive sight. Surprisingly for its size and magnificent appearance, it belonged to a private lord and not any royalty, as is the case with other similar castles.

Privately-owned castles in Britain, Pembroke included, were mainly used for residential purposes and as administration centres for the lords' territories.

Pembroke Castle was repeatedly extended through its history and has stonework spanning many periods.

As I've previously mentioned, the Normans turned their attention to Wales after defeating the English at the Battle of Hastings in 1066. However, their conquest of Wales was more fragmented.

Earl Roger de Montgomery entered West Wales from Shrewsbury in 1093 and constructed the initial castle at Pembroke, this would have been built from timber and was under the control of his son Arnulf.

Despite being besieged by the Welsh on two occasions, this castle became the base for commanding the surrounding area.

Norman King Henry I took possession of the castle in 1102, he increased Norman control and founded a town with a market and mint at the castle gate.

The Earldom of Pembroke was created for Gilbert de Clare in 1138 by King Stephen.

His son Richard, the second Earl of Pembroke, after playing an integral role in the conquest of Ireland, wed Eva, the daughter of the King of Leinster, and after the king's passing, became his successor. When Richard died, his daughter Isabel became his heiress. She stayed as a ward of King Henry II

This photograph was taken during a visit to Pembroke Castle, the birthplace of Henry VII. It shows part of the entrance and its stone defences. The photo was taken after entering the castle and looking back.

until he married her off to William Marshal, who due to the marriage, became Earl of Pembroke in 1189.

Pembrokeshire continued to be self-governing all the way up to the reign of Henry VIII.

Pembroke Castle.

The king's writ was only known in Pembrokeshire, when issued by the crown when the earldom became vacant. The earls were able to enforce their own justice and had their own courts.

William Marshal became a potent character in both medieval England and Wales.

He was a crusader, who was loyal to Henry II, a supporter to Henry's sons Richard I and John, he was even regent to Henry III during infancy.

At Pembroke Castle his legacy probably lies in the stone construction of the great keep and a fair amount of the inner ward.

As mentioned before, William was succeeded by five sons.

The eldest, William Marshal II, was a supporter of King John's successor Henry III and showed his loyalty by bringing over an Irish force to help subdue Prince Llywelyn ap Iorwerth and his Welsh uprising.

This resulted in an agreement by the king between William Marshal II and the Welsh prince, in which Llywelyn was given Cardigan and Carmarthen.

Next brother in line Richard was not in the best favour at the court of England. As a result, King Henry III refused the inheritance of the Marshal estates, causing Richard to lay siege to his own castle. In 1234, he was killed in Ireland and Gilbert became Earl of Pembroke.

He increased Pembroke Castle in both size and strength.

Gilbert was killed in 1241 during a jousting tournament when he fell off his horse and was succeeded by Walter, who died four years later. The last Marshal brother, Anselm, was earl for only a matter of days. Like his brothers, Anselm died childless perhaps fulfilling a curse by an Irish bishop whom the first William Marshal had wronged. The curse stated all his sons would die without children.

However, let's not forget the seven daughters of William Marshal. The properties were distributed amongst them.

The castle at Pembroke went to Joan, who married William de Valence, the half-brother of Henry II. Through their marriage he became Lord of Pembroke but was not formally made earl.

During this time when there was a threat of danger, any townspeople would huddle together inside the castle walls for protection. William was responsible for constructing the walls and towers around the outer ward.

In a peaceful period under Edward I, the townspeople asked for the fortification of the town of Pembroke in order not to have to rely on the castle; their Lord obliged by building three main gates and a postern. Only fragments of these remain today.

When William de Valence passed away in 1296, his son Aymer became the next Earl of Pembroke. Similar to his father he was a soldier, but also a diplomat.

He was triumphant over the Scots at Ruthven in 1306, however at Bannockburn eight years later, he shared in the defeat. He would later die in Paris whilst on an embassy mission to Charles IV.

There was a lot of building work carried out during the De Valence tenure at the castle, spanning around seventy years. The male line died with Aymer. His sister's son with husband John de Hastings, Laurence, became Earl of Pembroke, but he died before he could take possession.

His son John, served in France with the Black Prince, and he succeeded to become the second earl in the Hastings line. However, he was killed in France in 1375, and his son also John succeeded him.

He died in 1389 when only seventeen years of age, thus ending an inheritance blood line of around 280 years, back to when King Stephen created the earldom for Gilbert de Clare.

The earldom was now in the hands of the crown under Richard II, and going forward constables were appointed by the royal crown.

1400 saw another Welsh uprising, this time led by Owain Glyndŵr.

Pembroke Castle managed to avoid a siege when the constable at the time, Francis a Court, bought off Glyndŵr using a type of land tax scheme.

Richard II had recently been deposed by Henry Boilingbroke. This usurper would become King Henry IV.

His son Humphrey was given the title of Duke of Gloucester and when his brother Henry V succeeded their father, he made Humphrey Earl of Pembroke.

When Henry VI succeeded, Gloucester his uncle was not popular with Queen Margaret of Anjou, who imprisoned him. He died in 1447.

The half-brother of Henry VI, and son of Owain Tewdwr and Queen Catherine of France, Jasper Tudor was made Earl of Pembroke in 1454.

Jasper was the first to create more of a home than a fortress at Pembroke Castle.

His brother Edmund, Earl of Richmond, married Lady Margaret Beaufort.

Whilst the Wars of the Roses were happening Edmund sent a young and pregnant Margaret to Pembroke Castle so that she would be protected under his brother's roof.

Though Edmund died in 1456, on a visit to the castle, a couple of months later, Margaret gave birth to a son Henry Tewdwr, later known as Henry Tudor. The tower believed to have been his birthplace has been named the Henry VII Tower.

The child would grow up to be Earl of Richmond and defeat Richard III at Bosworth thus ending the Wars of the Roses. He had by right of victory, if not by descent, become King Henry VII of England and founder of the Tudor dynasty.

For some time following this period, the castle was quite peaceful, almost as if left to fall asleep without being given a role. It was still an impressive place that remained under the crown until the reign of James I who gifted the castle to someone in his favour and from there it remained a privately-owned estate.

Henry VII tower at Pembroke Castle.

Although there would come a time for the castle at Pembroke to awaken. This time for civil war.

South Wales was predominantly Royalist, although Pembroke Castle was fortified for the Parliamentarians.

Involved at Pembroke were three protagonists: the Mayor of Pembroke, John Poyer; Colonel Powell; and Major General Laugharne. The mayor provided the money for the defensive measures, while the other two prepared for the fight.

After the capture of Tenby by Royalist Lord Carberry, a siege was laid at Pembroke. Thanks to the Parliamentary forces landing via the sea at Milford Haven, the siege was unsuccessful.

The Parliamentarians then went on the offensive and took Haverfordwest, Tenby and Carew along with some other castles.

A strange occurrence happened in 1618 at Pembroke Castle, in terms of a turnaround. The Civil War was nearing completion, so Oliver Cromwell ordered the disbandment of the forces at Pembroke, however Laugharne refused.

Poyer did not want to give up his post as Military Governor and officers were sent over by Lord Fairfax in an attempt to resolve matters. They occupied the town but were evicted.

Poyer, Powell and Laugharne then declared their allegiance to the king, even winning over some old Parliamentarians.

This would have been a setback to Cromwell's success and the man himself arrived in Pembroke on 24 May 1648 and the castle was placed under siege till 11 July.

The Royalists had surrendered exhausted and hungry. Poyer, Laugharne and Powell were classed as traitors and were sent to be tried at the Tower. They were condemned to death, but ultimately, they were told only one of them would be shot; they drew lots, with Poyer being the unlucky man.

The order to destroy Pembroke Castle was then given by Cromwell. After a large amount of damage had been done, the castle was left to rot and be plundered.

In 1880, J.R. Cobb spent around three years repairing what he could, though after this attempt, nothing else was done until 1928.

Major General Sir Ivor Philipps bought the ruins and began a plan of restoration. As a result of this, it is possible for us today to explore the castle and get a real sense of what it was like in the Middle Ages.

After his death, the castle was inherited by the general's daughter, Mrs Basil Ramsden in 1959. She transferred the castle to six trustees, three being appointed by her family and the other three by the town council.

These trustees are represented by Major Ivor Ramsden, Sir Ivor's grandson.

Wogans Cavern that lays beneath Pembroke Castle.

Raglan Castle

Raglan Castle is another gorgeous castle to visit and has the wow factor as you approach thanks to its hexagonal tower design. The castle is attributed to Sir William ap Thomas, the son of a minor Welsh gentry family, who quickly revealed his ambition to become a man of importance and value in South Wales.

In 1421 he became the steward of the Lordship of Abergavenny and by 1426 William had been knighted by Henry VI. He thus went forward from here, known as the Blue Knight of Gwent.

He went on to become the chief steward of the Duke of York's estates within Wales from 1442 to 1443. He was also appointed as the Sheriff of

A photograph that I took on my approach to Raglan Castle.

Cardiganshire and Carmarthenshire in 1435, and by 1449, he had been appointed as Sheriff of Glamorgan.

William's influence was mainly confined to South Wales, even though he'd become a member of the military council of Richard, Duke of York who was Lord of Usk.

He had done enough by association, and provided the foundations with the House of York for his son William Herbert to build a position of power.

After his wife Elizabeth Bloet, who inherited Raglan from her father Sir John Bloet, passed away, William retained Raglan as a tenant of his stepson Lord Berkeley. In 1425, it was agreed that William could hold Raglan for the rest of his life.

William's second marriage was to another heiress, Gwladus, daughter of Dafydd Gam, who was an opponent of Owain Glyndŵr; and the widow of Sir Roger Vaughan of Bredwardine in Herefordshire.

Both her father and previous husband had fought with King Henry V as part of the Welsh contingent in France. They were both killed at the Battle of Agincourt in 1415. William had also fought which likely enhanced his standing after being awarded profits.

In 1432 he was able to purchase the Manor House at Raglan from the Berkeley family. From this time, he most likely started to build the castle as we see today.

Sir William ap Thomas passed away in 1445, his body was brought back to Wales and buried at the Benedictine Priory church at Abergavenny. He was succeeded by his eldest son, William Herbert.

He became even wealthier and more politically powerful than his father. Herbert was able to establish himself as the most important Welshman in South Wales and cemented his position with the new Yorkist king, Edward IV. He was destined to play a significant role within the state during the early years of Edward IVs reign.

Due to his short life he can historically speaking be overshadowed by the Lancastrian Jasper Tudor, the half-brother of Henry VI and the Earl of Pembroke, but it could be argued that he was one of, if not the most important Welshman of his generation.

He consolidated the family's rise to major power and great wealth, in a clever move, by claiming a fictional descent from Herbert ap Godwin, who was a son of King Henry I. This was even upheld by an inquest around 1461.

William Herbert, just like his father, served in France and was captured at the Battle of Formigny in 1450. His release was most likely laid in the form of a ransom.

He was knighted just two years later and appears to have consolidated his estates and established trade connections with places such as France during the 1450s.

In 1460 he became Sheriff of Glamorgan and Constable of Usk Castle in reward for not supporting the Yorkist cause in 1459 at the Rout of Ludford Bridge.

Herbert in 1461 adjoined himself to Edward, Earl of March, who was the son of Richard, the Duke of York.

In the years 1455-87, which became known as the Wars of the Roses, Herbert was the greatest Welshman to support Edward's bid for the throne.

In a battle that proved to be a decisive Yorkist victory, Herbert was instrumental in the defeat of the Lancastrian troops led by Jasper Tudor.

A mere month later, Edward then ascended to the throne as king. As a thank you for his support, Edward IV made the loyal and trustworthy William Chief Justice and Chamberlain of South Wales.

In the very same year, William would be appointed Baron Herbert of Raglan.

The Lancastrian threat in Wales during the 1460s probably caused Herbert great concern.

His influence would eventually extend to North Wales as he became accountable for the military operations against the Lancastrians in the whole of Wales.

His titles did not stop there: in 1467 he was made a Knight of the Garter; and Chief Justice of North Wales.

Henry Tudor was brought under the custody of William Herbert and his wife so that the child could be brought up at Raglan Castle, and as we know this child went on to become King Henry VII and founded the Tudor dynasty.

Herbert was now in a good position to create the palace fortress at Raglan that would reflect the status of the man he had become.

The castle most likely became an administrative hub for the newly created Marcher Lordship of Raglan that had been brought about in 1465. This was acted independently from the Lordship of Usk and would be free of royal officials' interference.

It shows Herbert's importance to the new king as this was the only Marcher lordship to be created in Wales after 1284.

His last accolade came in 1468 in the form of the Earldom of Pembroke. This was given by King Edward IV in reward for Herbert's capture of Harlech Castle in North Wales, the last remaining Lancastrian stronghold in both England and Wales.

Earl William was the first member of Welsh gentry to enter English peerage. A Welsh country squire had turned himself into an English magnate, with a good annual income.

William Herbert was able to carry on what his father had started at Raglan Castle, and he did so on a grand scale. The current appearance of the castle is mainly due to him, other than perhaps parts from the Tudor and Jacobean rebuilding periods.

Herbert constructed a spectacular new gatehouse and approach to the castle; he also created courts on either side of the previous great hall range to serve in the running of the house and to provide accommodation for residents and guests.

Unfortunately for Herbert he was not to enjoy his palatial style fortress for long. He was defeated in July 1469, at the Battle of Edgecote. He and his brother were captured by the Earl of Warwick, known as the kingmaker. Warwick was a deserter of the Yorkist cause, and he executed the men in Northampton just a day after their capture. Even in this time this was considered an arbitrary act.

Herbert's body was brought back to South Wales and laid to rest in the Cistercian abbey at Tintern, the patronage of which had been passed to him along with Chepstow in 1468.

His heir from his marriage to Anne Devereux, William the younger, was just fourteen years old when his father died. Raglan stayed within the hands of his mother whilst he was a minor; she later resided at Chepstow, where she had been granted the castle by the terms of her late husband's will.

The execution of William Herbert the elder in 1469 marked the end of the family's grand influence in national affairs, despite his heir's marriage in 1466 to Mary Woodville, sister of the queen.

William the younger in 1479 was relieved of the Earldom of Pembroke so that King Edward IV could give the honour to his own son the Prince of Wales. In exchange, he was given the Earldom of Huntingdon, and he would later become chamberlain to the prince, and even regained his position as Chief Justice of South Wales under Richard III.

When he passed in 1491, with there being no male heir, the Herbert barony passed to his daughter Elizabeth.

For seven years, however, the castle would be under the care of Sir Walter Herbert, the earl's younger brother.

With Henry Tudor landing at Milford Haven in 1485, he quickly aligned with the Tudor dynasty, after previously being a prominent House of York supporter.

In 1502, Walter Herbert entertained the king's wife at the castle; she belonged to the Woodville family on her mother's side thus having connections with Raglan Castle, as indeed did Henry VII himself.

Walter Herbert died in 1507 and the king passed Raglan to his wife Anne. But after her remarriage, it appears the castle was granted to Elizabeth and her husband Sir Charles Somerset, the son of Henry Beaufort, who had married in 1492.

Sir Charles was a keen supporter of Henry VII and he was Lord Chamberlain to both him and his successor, Henry VIII.

He became designated Baron Herbert of Raglan, Chepstow and Gower, by the right of inheritance of his wife.

Sir Charles also took part in the first military expedition to France by Henry VIII and was created Earl of Worcester as a result. He died in 1526. He is buried in Beaufort Chapel, within St George's Chapel at Windsor Castle.

He was succeeded by his eldest son Henry, though Henry was lacking in his father's ability. He was given a number of monastic properties, such as Tintern Abbey in 1537, this coming after the suppression of the monasteries.

By 1546, most of the lead from the abbey was purchased by Henry, probably for building work at sites like Raglan and Chepstow.

He passed away just three years later and he is buried at St Mary's Church in Chepstow.

He was followed by William Somerset the third Earl of Worcester and later his son Edward. These men showed better ability, had ambition, were cultured and wealthy with prominent roles at court. It was during their period of succession that Raglan saw its last big building phase.

William Somerset managed to hold positions at the courts of three different sovereigns: Edward VI, Mary and Elizabeth I. He earned particular distinction in the Elizabethan period where he undertook some business abroad on the queen's behalf and by 1570 he had been made a Knight of the Garter. When he passed away in 1589, he became the first of his family to be laid to rest in Raglan Church. Most of his monument was quite damaged during the fighting in the Civil War.

When William inherited the castle, it apparently had barely been altered since his ancestors of the Herbert line had built it a century before. He made improvements in the hall and service ranges to be in-keeping with the social needs of the day. His work can be noted by the use of dark red sandstone and not the pale yellow that would have been used earlier.

William's son Edward was regarded as a brilliant horseman. This was confirmed when he was given the royal office of Master of the Horse. Even though he was Roman Catholic, Edward was a favourite of Queen Elizabeth I. He even remained in such favour with the succession of James I, where he was Earl Marshal at the coronation and as Lord Great Chamberlain when Charles I became King.

The work that can be attributed to Edward at the castle includes such things as the two fireplaces above the buttery. He continued to develop the

Ruins at Raglan Castle.

amazing gardens that had been started by his father. Edward also added the moat walk around the great tower.

With the appearance of antiquities becoming more and more common, the niches were decorated in coloured plaster, shell work and housed statues of Roman Emperors.

Henry inherited Raglan in 1628 and thus became the fifth Earl of Worcester. In the early part of the seventeenth century, the approach to the main gatehouse was enhanced, firstly with an addition of a white gate and later with an outer enclosure in which a carpark now stands.

A second gate was constructed, the red gate made out of brick, on the line of the wall that overlooked a big pool crossed by the main approach to the castle.

Leading up to the Civil War, Raglan was spectacular, although within about ten years this would all come to an end with the defeat of Charles I, for whom Henry had declared his support.

At the Battle of Naseby in June 1645, the Royalist army was defeated practically sealing the fate of King Charles I. Though only a small number of isolated Royalist resistance pockets remained, the war managed to continue until 1646.

On 16 August 1646, Pendennis in Cornwall surrendered, and Raglan was to follow a mere three days later. Thus, the Civil War came to an end, though Harlech Castle managed to hold out until March 1647.

Henry, Earl of Worcester had held the castle at Raglan for the king, who made him Marquess of Worcester in 1643. He was a staunch Royalist, and it is believed that he personally supported the garrison at Raglan financially to around £40,000. Apparently, the garrison in 1646 consisted of 800 people.

On more than one occasion King Charles I was entertained at the castle during the fighting and Henry is estimated to have contributed £1,000,000 to the royal cause.

Up to date defences were created to help the castle withstand a siege. Fortifications in Europe were now built lower than the medieval fortresses in a bid to combat artillery fire.

The key though was the angle bastion, an arrow-shaped gun platform which enabled troops to flank the ground in front of the defences between two bastions and therefore earthworks were constructed in front of the castle.

Raglan's extension of defences allowed the large garrison to mount an effective defence.

After the surrender of the castle at Raglan to the Parliamentarians in 1646, an old Henry was taken as prisoner to London, along with his doctor and servants, but he passed away not long afterwards. He did receive a state burial and was laid to rest at Beaufort Chapel at Windsor Castle.

Some deliberate destruction at the castle added to the damage already inflicted by the siege.

Raglan Castle, along with other property, was confiscated, and the Lordship of Chepstow was bestowed upon Oliver Cromwell.

Henry Somerset, the third Marquess of Worcester from 1667, was able to restore a number of the family's former possessions, including the castle before the end of the Commonwealth.

His family still owned a Tudor mansion called Troy House on the outskirts of Monmouth, but when the restoration of the crown saw Charles II take the throne to rule with parliament, Somerset began his rebuilding.

He started in Gloucestershire with Badminton House. This manor had been purchased by the fourth Earl in 1608.

In the 1680s, he rebuilt Troy House on a large scale as the Monmouthshire seat of his heir. In 1673 he completed the Great Castle House in Monmouth, after his appointment as Lord President of the Council of Wales and the Marches the previous year.

Any plans to restore Raglan Castle to its former glory seem to have been abandoned after this, although the village church did remain as a place of burial for the family until as late as 1710.

From 1682, Henry was granted a dukedom and his family bestowed with the title of Dukes of Beaufort.

Just as had happened at other castles, Raglan was used for its building materials in the later part of the seventeenth and eighteenth centuries.

The Somerset family had retained some of their items in 1646 and later, for example, there is a portrait of William, third Earl of Worcester at Badminton House which is believed to have hung at Raglan.

The castle was then set to become a ruin, rustic bridges and seats were added and even a guidebook. Small repairs were completed during the ensuing years.

A photograph from inside Raglan Castle.

By 1938, the tenth Duke of Beaufort placed the castle under the guardianship of the HM Commissioners of Works and for around twenty years after the Second World War a large project of conservation was carried out.

Raglan Castle is now under the care of Cadw on behalf of the Welsh Assembly.

Dinefwr Castle and Dryslwyn Castle

On my first visit to Dinefwr Castle, as I approached the remains of this magnificent fortification, I was able to see how its position provided an exceptional defensive advantage as it sits upon a long ridge; similarly, this would also be true for Dinefwr's neighbouring castle Dryslwyn which is placed upon a rocky knoll.

Dinefwr was the principal court of the Kingdom of Deheubarth.

Dryslwyn Castle, with the picturesque Tywi Valley.

Due to records from Brut y Tywysogion, we know that Rhys ap Gruffudd took Cantref Mawr and Dinefwr Castle in 1165. He retained these up until his passing in 1197.

Lord Rhys was the figurehead of the Kingdom of Deheubarth with Dinefwr as its main seat. He is remembered as one of the greatest Welsh leaders of the twelfth century, who withstood the might of the Anglo-Norman Lords of the March, even being supported on occasion by King Henry II.

Lord Rhys took advantage of Henry's conciliatory policy after 1171 in order to maintain stable authority for years. The kingdom was then able to prosper in a time of relative peace and harmony. His patronage and self-assured governance were beneficial to Welsh culture.

Lord Rhys was a realist who was not concerned with taking on the mighty Anglo-Norman Lords of the Southern March; neither did he attempt to influence the rulers of Gwynedd and Powys.

He was not shy of military action; he had previously been forced to restore the authority of his lineage in a kingdom that had been broken by Anglo-Norman aggression.

Over about twenty years or so he was able to bring the lands of Ystrad Tywi, Ceredigion and parts of Dyfed back under a single power and as a result brought a vast part of the ancient Kingdom of Deheubarth under his control.

He took the fortress at Cardigan and mostly either built or rebuilt the fortifications at Llandovery, Rhayader and Nevern on his borders. All of his conquests and deeds came from good common sense.

These conquests were solidified by the negotiation of marriages, so binding himself to the native rulers.

He also married two of his daughters off to Norman lords and his son and heir to the daughter of the mighty Anglo-Norman Marcher house of Braose. Rhys was securing the borders of his territory.

Deheubarth by 1180 had been restored and was the premier kingdom in Wales, even under the overall authority of an English monarch.

We cannot know entirely what Rhys' castle at Dinefwr would have looked like due to centuries of extensive rebuilding and repairs. Its layout may have not been too dissimilar to what you can see today.

After the passing of Lord Rhys in 1197, there was a dispute over the succession at Deheubarth. It was most likely that Lord Rhys had intended that the kingdom go to his eldest legitimate son Gruffudd ap Rhys, but his other sons Maelgwyn ap Rhys and Rhys Gryg challenged for the throne.

A struggle was set to follow and in the prolonged fighting, castles were captured and recaptured during this sibling conflict. With Gruffudd passing away young, his sons Rhys Ieuanc and Owain continued in the struggle.

In 1204, Maelgwyn lost Llandovery Castle and Dinefwr Castle to his nephews.

The struggle continued nearly ten years later in 1213, where Rhys Gryg had to defend Dinefwr Castle against his nephew Rhys Ieuanc.

In the attack, Ieuanc had men scale the castle walls and eventually took the castle.

Eventually it was due to the power of Llywelyn ab Iorwerth, the Prince of Gwynedd, that an agreement was drawn up.

In 1216, the princes were summoned by Llywelyn to Aberdyfi urging them to split the kingdom into three factions.

The South East went to Maelgwyn, and was awarded to Rhys Gryg, this included the castles at Dinefwr and Dryslwyn; and Rhys Ieuanc and Owain were given Ceredigion. They were now all rulers although be it in a now diminished manner. Deheubarth was not to recover the status it had grown accustomed to under the rule of Lord Rhys.

In spite of this both Dinefwr and Dryslwyn in these decades attained their potent masonry construction, although both would eventually succumb to King Edward I.

After Dinefwr and the lordship over the Ystrad Tywi had been given to Rhys Gryg in 1219, his position was once again strengthened by his marriage to Matilda de Clare, who was the sister of Gilbert de Clare, the Earl of Gloucester.

Though Rhys could never fully relax, Llywelyn ap Iorwerth was required to pay homage to the king in return for the peace and the ownership of the crucial fortifications of Carmarthen and Cardigan and he had to persuade the magnates throughout Wales to do the same.

However, Rhys Gryg strongly refused to do so, although when Llywelyn sent forth an army, ultimately ending in a battle between forces from Gwynedd and Deheubarth at Carmarthen Bridge, Rhys yielded.

Around thirteen years of relative peace followed.

Up until his death Rhys was subservient to the king and a supporter of Llywelyn. Being under the king's protection as a vassal, Rhys probably had the time and opportunity to rebuild afresh.

On his passing in 1233, his lands were divided up. Dinefwr was awarded to his elder son Rhys Mechyll and the east of the Ystrad Tywi; whilst the west most likely being ruled from Dryslwyn, went to his younger son Maredudd ap Rhys.

In a similar manner to what had gone before, both men paid homage to King Henry III. They became free of their subordination to the House of Gwynedd after Llywelyn died in 1240.

Rhys Mechyll's son Rhys Fychan succeeded him, and he along with his uncle sided with Dafydd the son of Llywelyn in his efforts to regain native control cross Wales. However, this came to an end with Dafydd's death in 1246.

The loss of Dinefwr to the English was a punishment doled out to Rhys, although he was re-established at Dinefwr by 1248, after he recognized the jurisdiction of the king's court at Carmarthen.

Maredudd was able to retain Dryslwyn.

The territory of Ystrad Tywi over the next twenty-five years was under the influence of Llywelyn ab Iorwerth's grandson.

The relationship between Rhys Fychan and Maredudd had become strained, most likely due to the continued arguments over the territories that they ruled.

After having the support from the Royal commander at Carmarthen, Rhys Fychan secured the upper hand with Maredudd. As a result, Maredudd aligned with the cause of Llywelyn.

In 1256 Llywelyn invaded Ystrad Tywi with Maredudd at his side. Rhys Fychan was completely ousted, resulting in Maredudd becoming Lord of Ystrad Tywi.

Rhys Fychan out of desperation turned towards the king's commander, Stephen Bauzan, who headed an army that marched into the Tywi Valley to re-establish Rhys's power.

During the advance to Dinefwr, Rhys Fychan deserted and suffered a crushing defeat at Cymerau.

In the summer of the same year near enough the whole of the southwest was under Welsh control, placing the Lordships of Pembroke under threat.

Llywelyn now needed a reconciliation between Rhys Fychan and Maredudd.

The settlement that Llywelyn contemplated meant that Dinefwr Castle and most of the land next to it was given back to Rhys Fychan, with Maredudd in a more confined lordship centred at Dryslwyn.

Maredudd was unhappy that his support of Llywelyn had not rewarded him in the way that he had expected causing him to turn back towards the king. Llywelyn did not take this lightly; he captured Maredudd and convicted him of disloyalty in 1258.

He was imprisoned at Criccieth Castle, being freed three years later, but relations with Llywelyn were now soured beyond repair.

In 1267, the Treaty of Montgomery saw the king grant to the now Prince of Wales Llywelyn the allegiance of the other princes of Wales.

Maredudd's homage to Henry III was denied and in 1270 the king agreed with Llywelyn that he would be bestowed with Maredudd's homage, under the condition of a payment of 5,000 marks.

Henry III was persuaded to do this by his son Edward, who wanted to use the money on the expenses of the crusade that he was about to embark upon.

Just as before the princes of Southwest Wales ruled, but only under the agreement from the House of Gwynedd.

In 1271 Maredudd passed away at his castle at Dryslwyn and he was laid to rest in Whitland Abbey. A mere three weeks later, Rhys Fychan passed away at his castle in Dinefwr and was laid to rest at Tally Abbey. His successor at Dinefwr was his son Rhys Wyndod and Dryslwyn passed to Rhys ap Maredudd, the son of Maredudd.

The following year in 1272, King Henry died, and Edward I took to the throne.

Llywelyn had repeatedly defied the new king, and had exhausted his patience.

Payne de Chaworth was ordered by the king to gather an army at Carmarthen.

Parts of the south crumbled quickly in the summertime of 1277.

Rhys ap Maredudd sought terms and was able to retain some districts and keep Dryslwyn.

A month later, Rhys Wyndod submitted to the king and deserted away from Llywelyn. However, he was unable to keep Dinefwr.

The symbolic seat of Dinefwr was confiscated by the king and came under the custody of the justiciar of West Wales Bogo de Knovill.

Both princes felt aggrieved by the treatment they had received. Rhys ap Maredudd felt that after being the first to submit in the war of 1277, he should have been better rewarded, as it had proved a great benefit to the English campaign.

Rhys Wyndod was in a new predicament; he was now involved in legal action that was brought before the royal justices by John Giffard, the Lord of Llandovery, who claimed some of the prince's inheritance.

Rhys ap Maredudd supported King Edward, but Rhys Wyndod was left feeling angry about his treatment during the judicial proceedings and felt resentful regarding the king's failure to secure the prince justice.

He had his reasons for joining the rebellion of Dafydd ap Gruffudd, who was the Prince of Wales in 1282. After he had been forced to submit to royal forces which could now use Dinefwr as their base for operations in Ystrad Tywi, he eventually forfeited his inheritance. Along with some other princes of Deheubarth and Powys, he was exiled to Gwynedd and later sent to the Tower of London and placed in lifetime imprisonment.

He had seen the death of Llywelyn ap Gruffudd in a battle near Builth in 1282, and then Dafydd's capture and death via execution.

During the aftermath, Rhys ap Maredudd, now the only descendant of Lord Rhys, had a degree of power and was part of a small number of Welsh princes that had remained loyal to the royal crown, and he was rewarded with lands.

Although once again he was denied Dinefwr Castle and further so in 1263, he was requested to accept that he had no rights to the mighty fortification.

In the following year, Edward I ordained a new system of government for the crown lands in Wales, through the Statute of Wales. This involved the provision of the combination of his power in the southwestern counties of Cardigan and Carmarthen, previously created by his predecessor.

Rhys ap Maredudd quickly became entangled in disputes with Robert de Tibetot, the new justiciar of West Wales. In June 1287, these disputes worsened. Rhys ap Maredudd captured the fortresses of Dinefwr, Carreg Cennen and Llandovery. The constables were murdered and most of the defenders were left for dead.

The response from the English was swift. A large army of more than 11,000 men from various parts of England and Wales was raised and marched into Carmarthen to congregate under Earl Edmund, the king's cousin. They set out and laid siege to Dryslwyn Castle, the site of Rhys' defensive headquarters.

There is a lot of documentation regarding the siege, so we are able to have a good understanding of this event.

The things we know are, that in response to Rhys's revolt in 1287, there was a well-coordinated English reaction. Edward I was not in the country at the time and his regent Earl Edmund had to take charge.

Earl Edmund was at the head of the army with around 4,000 men, some of whom had been raised from England while others had been sourced locally under Robert de Tibetot.

The earl's troops were joined by a force of 6,700, consolidated under Reginald Grey, who set out from Chester, and Roger L'Estrange, who set out from Montgomery.

The combined army assembled on the floor of the valley in front of Dryslwyn Castle around 15 August and the siege began.

A lot of the men drafted under Reginald Grey were from the building works of Edward I's castles of North Wales. These were able craftsmen and along with others, built a trebuchet that was able to hurl large stones at Dryslwyn's walls. It was constructed out of timber, ropes, hides and lead. Twenty quarrymen and twenty-four carters were employed to move and shape the stone balls that were thrown at the castle from the trebuchet.

The besiegers in addition to this attempted to undermine the castle's walls. The records state they were able to bring down a big section near the chapel block, although archaeological evidence is suggestive that this happened on the other side of the castle, facing towards the town area.

Dryslwyn was captured by 5 September. Rhys ap Maredudd escaped, but his wife and son were captured.

In archaeological excavations of this area, two stone balls over sixteen inches in diameter were found that had been thrown by the trebuchet. Many smaller stones were also recovered, along with arrowheads, links of chain mail, slingshots and a spearhead.

Many of the recovered arrowheads had long sharp points in order to penetrate armour and chain mail.

Dinefwr Castle had been retaken, Rhys had fled, but after just a few years of further resistance, Rhys was caught in 1292 and was executed at York accused of treason.

In just over a decade the new monarch had destroyed the power of the Prince of Wales.

From 1287, both Dinefwr and Dryslwyn served as royal castles and were in the custody of a constable of the crown.

Surviving records show us an indication of the destiny of these magnificent fortresses.

A set of accounts for Dryslwyn provides us with the information that between 1287 and 1289, the constable at the time, Alan de Plucknet, had made a payment of nearly £130 to fix the repairs that had been caused by the siege. This was paid to masons and quarrymen. A payment of £109 for the construction of the new mill is also recorded, being paid to carpenters, smiths and charcoal burners.

Also £36 was paid for the felling of woodland near the castle, the renovation of ditches and for some other minor work.

At Dinefwr the expense that was spent on repairing the castle appears smaller. Accounts by the justiciar of West Wales around the start of the century provide us with an insight into life in these military garrisons. Food supplies like grain, honey, salt, wine and meat had to be brought in from the surrounding area and sent over the country in order to feed the garrisons, consisting of twenty-four men that were under a constable.

During much of the 1290s, Dinefwr Castle was held by John Giffard, but in 1310-11 Dinefwr was given to Edmund Hakelut for life and he secured the constableship for his son also named Edmund.

However, this long tenure was interrupted in 1317 by Edward II who gave both Dinefwr and Dryslwyn to Hugh Despenser.

Dinefwr had been badly damaged by a fire in 1316 during a Welsh revolt. It was further damaged in an attack by Marcher lords in 1321 and large amounts were spent on building repairs after the castle was returned to Edmund Hakelut following the fall of Hugh Despenser in 1326.

Dryslwyn also saw attacks in 1321 and they most likely caused a lot of damage. In 1338-39 repairs are recorded as happening to a block of rooms on the west side of the king's hall. Some modifications during the same time were made to the hall, this included a new window and doorway.

A survey that was undertaken in 1343 for Edward the Black Prince, tells us that the great tower at Dinefwr was nearing collapse and would cost around £139 to repair.

In spite of the repairs in 1338-39, Dryslwyn seems to have been in a poorer state.

Inspectors of the Black Prince estimated a sum of £342 for needed repairs, including restoring the inner bailey wall, the great tower and the tower called Appeltour.

However, at neither of the castles are there any records of large-scale rebuilding being carried out on the defences in the later part of the fourteenth century.

Some reports also inform us that there were new service rooms and bake houses, but the sad conclusion was that the castles were being to become neglected. They were kept reasonably comfortable and intact by their custodians, but the base of royal authority and power in the southeast now sat at Carmarthen and Cardigan.

Near the start of the fifteenth century, there was a new Welsh champion named Owain Glyndŵr and he would lead the English to regret any complacency with the castles.

In the summertime of 1403, Glyndŵr arrived in person in the Tywi Valley and various royal servants found themselves in a plight.

On 4 July, Rhys ap Gruffudd surrendered to the Welsh rebels.

A force led by Henry Don, along with his son and Gwilym ap Philip, had started a siege of Dinefwr from 2 July.

The Constable at Dinefwr was John Havard, who feared that he would have to abandon the castle and flee for Brecon, if relief was not forthcoming, although perhaps astonishingly the isolated fortress, surrounded by an enemy force, held out against an intense assault.

Eventually after ten days of fighting, the besieging force withdrew. It would be some three years later before English authority would be restored in the Tywi Valley.

There is a record of £89 being spent at Dinefwr Castle on repairs and the construction of new buildings.

However, at Dryslwyn, the Glyndŵr rebellion could have led to the final abandonment of the fortress here. There are no surviving records of any repairs at the castle, and it is not known that the fortress played any further part in any military operations. Archaeological evidence suggests that the castle was deliberately destroyed sometime in the first half of the fifteenth century.

After the latest period of disruption, there were new constables appointed to Dinefwr Castle, the first being Hugh Standish in 1408, followed by his brother Christopher in 1411.

Looking up at the ruins of Dryslywn Castle.

When Christopher died in 1425, the constableship was awarded to his son, Roland, a military man who was often engaged in foreign wars, so he passed the responsibility of running the castle to Gruffudd ap Nicolas. He was a descendant of a notable Welsh family, and he quickly rose in influence and power. He gained the trust of busy officials, who used him to deputize for their administrative affairs. He managed to gradually gain many landholdings in Cardiganshire and Carmarthenshire and even garnered influence within the local government.

It could be argued that it was Gruffudd who constructed the first Newton House at Dinefwr, as a comfortable home, away from the medieval castle.

He was a Lancastrian supporter who found his power curbed on the outbreak of the Wars of the Roses.

In 1456 he was devoid of Dinefwr, and he died four years later.

Dinefwr Castle would later be restored to the descendants of Gruffudd ap Nicholas. His heir Thomas allegedly lived at Abermarlais, the family estate of his wealthy wife.

His son Rhys ap Thomas was a keen supporter of Henry Tudor and assisted him in his invasion at Milford Haven and was knighted for his service in 1485, at the Battle of Bosworth. He secured Dinefwr for life and became justiciar of South Wales.

After Henry VII's passing, Rhys was still in good favour with the new king Henry VIII. With his main residence at Abermarlais, he maintained the house at Dinefwr. However, it is probable that the old castle continued in its slow decline into a romantic and picturesque ruin.

Dinefwr also boasts beautiful parkland.

The descendants of Sir Rhys ap Thomas were the Rice family, and from the mid-seventeenth century onwards, continuing generations of the family were appreciative of the significance of the romantic ruin and the castle as a viewing point from which to admire Dinefwr Park.

George Rice, along with wife Cecil in the 1750s, took on the new fashionable concept of the time that gardens should be reflective of the surrounding landscape. The trend was a much more naturalistic interpretation, rather than straight lines and angles. Together they began creating one of the finest parks in Britain.

There are some records of the acquisition of land, hedge removal and the removal of buildings to the east of Newton House.

Luckily for the Rice family, Dinefwr already had some essential components in place, mature trees in the deer park and flowing water.

Lancelot 'Capability' Brown visited the site in 1775 and stated: 'I wish my journey may prove of use to this place which if it should, will be very flattering to me. Nature has been truly bountiful and art has done no harm.'

As the century continued, trends moved to the picturesque, a more rugged and wild approach to landscape design.

William Gilpin was an advocate of this method and was inspired by what he saw at Dinefwr, leading the Rice family to be praised for a landscape that they had done little to enhance. The park we can see today is relatively

Walking at Dinefwr you spot Newton House through the trees.

unchanged. Looking from the castle's towers you are still able to admire and appreciate the achievements of George and his wife.

Towards the west and southwest, spaces are enclosed by continuous woodland and knolls with framed views; whilst to the east there are rolling landforms with planting in regimented clumps.

There is some intermingling that occurs with parts of woodland extending the picturesque elements towards Llandeilo.

Curving drives and circular paths offer amazing views towards the castle and Newton House and the river valley.

The National Trust, along with its partners Cadw and the Wildlife Trust of South and West Wales, have restored and enhanced the design from the eighteenth century. There has been the removal of modern fences; driveways and paths have been restored; vistas have been reinstalled; and trees planted.

Also, the improvements on the biodiversity will be beneficial to the wildlife, but will also help to restore the colour and texture of the grass swards.

Newton House is also open to the public, and is well worth a look around. Inside you will be able to find an explanation of key parts of the park that encourage visitors to explore and enjoy this truly beautiful place.

Above: Newton House at Dinefwr.

Left: A side photograph of the beautiful Newton House.

The gardens of Newton house, against the backdrop of Dinefwr.

Both Dinefwr and Dryslwyn by the later eighteenth century had become ruins beloved by Romantics. People travelled across Britain at the time and were moved by the aesthetics.

It was defined by William Gilpin as 'that peculiar kind of beauty which is agreeable in a picture'.

The juxtaposition between the ruinous castle and the great Newton House with its beautiful gardens formed the ideal subject for most, though an attempt was made to improve Dinefwr's silhouette and provide a lookout point.

By 1775 Lancelot 'Capability' Brown had been commissioned to provide advice around landscaping.

When artist John Warwick Smith made a visit to Dinefwr in 1796-97, a fire had destroyed the summer house and in his picture of Dinefwr you can see it with ruinous parts.

In a landscape painting by J.M.W. Turner, the castle isn't shown in much detail, but concentrates more on the ruinous bridge with the castle almost faded into the background.

In a picture by Paul Sandby in 1779, the outline of the ruinous castle is portrayed in contrast against the calm, landscaped park, with cattle, deer and an aristocrat upon horseback.

While not that popular with artists, possibly due to it early abandonment and collapse, Dinefwr was a popular site for picnics during the eighteenth and nineteenth centuries and porcelain fragmentation has been excavated from around its gatehouse.

It was not just artists that went in search of the picturesque, but writers and poets also. John Dyer's poem *Grongar Hill* describes Dinefwr.

Interest in Dinefwr and Dryslwyn began to decline around 1830. The neglect led to even more collapse and a slow covering of debris, though some periodic repairs did happen at Dinefwr Castle.

The ruins of Dryslwyn Castle were taken under the guardianship of the state in 1980 and a programme of conservation and excavation was carried out over the next fifteen years. Conservation of the remains of the Dinefwr site started slightly later.

Both Dinefwr and Dryslwyn are now under the care of Cadw and maintained through them.

A photograph of the Dinefwr landscape that is opposite Newton House.

Laugharne Castle

Laugharne Castle is located on the mouth of the River Taf, originally built in 1116 as a small stronghold.

The castle throughout its history was repeatedly captured and retaken.

Sir Guy De Brian is the first recorded holder of the castle, in the early fourteenth century.

Sir John Perot was the owner during Henry VIII's reign, who incorporated most of the castle into a fortified mansion.

This castle is on my list because it links back to my first chapter on Dylan Thomas. You can see this castle during Dylan's Birthday Walk and it is the castle that is mentioned in his poem *October*.

Aberystwyth Castle

Gilbert de Clare built the first castle at Llanfarian in the Ystwyth Valley, about two miles from the current site. The original construction would have been a modest structure made of timber and stone that was attacked and rebuilt often.

Cardiganshire was given to Rhys ap Gruffudd by Henry II in 1171. He was a self-proclaimed ruler of Wales. Following his passing, a family feud broke out with one of his sons, Maelgwyn, seizing the territory.

In 1207, Maelgwyn destroyed the castle out of concern that Llywelyn the Great would attack, but the castle would later be rebuilt.

The family dispute would continue for several years regarding the ownership of the castle. However, in 1215, Llywelyn the Great would capture Cardigan Castle and eventually would take the possession of Aberystwyth Castle.

This castle would go on to be captured and then recaptured several times over the next sixteen years. In the late thirteenth century, Edward I built the castle that stands on the current site.

Aberystwyth Castle overlooks Cardigan Bay and it was to become one of the strongest defences of the West Coast.

In 1404, Owain Glyndŵr took the town and its castle, although Prince Henry's forces would take it just three years later. Glyndŵr forces reclaimed it, but yet again it went back under English control.

In the Tudor period, the castles of Wales and their occupants did enjoy a time of stability.

The castle saw action during the first English Civil war between 1642 and 1646. Much like other Welsh castles the owners here supported the Royalists, until the forced surrender to Rice Powell a Parliamentarian colonel, after a siege in 1646.

For showing support to the Royalist cause, Oliver Cromwell gave the order for the castle to be demolished in 1647.

Cilgerran Castle

This castle stands above the River Teifi, and for that reason the castle provides some lovely views of the river surrounded by greenery.

A view of the surrounding area from the castle ruins of Cilgerran.

In 1093, the Normans conquered West Wales which was under Rhys ap Tewdwr, the ruler of the Kingdom of Deheubarth.

Whilst advancing west, the Normans built castles in Cardigan, Carmarthen and Pembroke in order to take control of their territory.

Cilgerran Castle was built by Gerald de Windsor, who was one of Henry I's Marcher lords.

However, Lord Rhys would capture the castle in 1165, during the reign of Henry II, a year after the fall of Cardigan Castle during the advance through West Wales.

In 1204, Earl of Pembroke, William Marshal, would capture Cilgerran Castle.

During the uprising of Llywelyn the Great, Pembrokeshire and this castle were recaptured by his army.

The ownership of the castle changed again in 1223, this time into the hands of William Marshal's eldest son.

The castle was extensively rebuilt, during a time of peace, in order to take full advantage of its location.

Whilst the castle did not play a significant role in Llywelyn's uprising, there was a good victory for him in a battle that was fought nearby.

Cilgerran Castle stayed under the Marshal family's control until the passing of. Anselm in 1245.

The next owners of the castle were the De Cantelupes, who occupied the castle till the end of the fourteenth century.

However, they neglected the castle and by 1275 a lot of the furnishings had either been stolen or removed. Sadly by 1325 the castle was classed as a ruin and it was recommended it be demolished.

However, with Edward III fearing an invasion after the defeat of an English force by the Spanish fleet in 1372, he ordered the castle to be both repaired and strengthened.

The castle would once again suffer from considerable damage to its infrastructure in 1405 when it was captured by Owain Glyndŵr's army.

When the Wars of the Roses took place, the castle became the property of the Tudors.

Henry VIII in the 1536 Act of Union abolished the Marcher lordships and the rights of the castle were granted to the Vaughan family, which would last well into the seventeenth century.

This castle's great advantage was the steep slopes that surrounded it on three sides. Its design was typical of the time with a motte and a bailey defended by a ditch.

The castle has two large towers, with a gatehouse and an outer ward guarded by a large ditch.

Ruins at Cilgerran Castle.

Hay Castle

It is believed that this castle was built by a knight named Revell in about 1100. It would have consisted of a motte and bailey and been strengthened in the thirteenth century with wall extensions and a gateway.

During a period of relative peace within the Welsh borders after the removal of the Marchers in the sixteenth century and the Act of Union, Hay Castle became a more domestic setting.

It was possibly originally a small Tudor house that was adjoined to the keep, which then became the larger Jacobean mansion that you are still able to see today.

Analysis of some of the timbers from the roof date the mansion to being built around 1640.

It has a gorgeous brick chimney that stands out against the pretty backdrop of Hay's skyline.

The castle was home to the Lords of Hay and Joseph Bailey made it his residence as Lord Glanusk in the nineteenth century. He made some alterations, including adding the coach house and a carriage drive.

His cousin William Latham Bevan along with his family came to live at Hay Castle in 1845. He was the Vicar of Hay, but there was no vicarage in the town at the time.

When the Bevans vacated, the Dowager Lady Glanusk returned. An article from 1914 in *Country Life* showed the renovations that were made for it to be a more suitable place for her residency.

With Lady Glanusk's passing in 1938, the residence was rented out and in 1939 when a huge fire broke out, the property was in the hands of the Guinness family. The fire devastated the eastern section and half the building was left in ruins without a roof.

It stood empty during the Second World War, but was then bought by Edward Vernon Tuson who had married into the Studt fairground family, and you could say 'collected' castles.

Around 1961 the property was bought by Richard Booth, who was fundamental in the idea of making Hay the world's first book town. In the quiet, peaceful market town of Hay, he seized the opportunity to establish second hand bookstores. He did this by purchasing books in bulk from America, transporting them in lorries to be delivered to the castle.

The castle began to act like a hub for the increasing number of bookstores that Booth had helped encourage to open. By 1977 he had the idea of declaring Hay as an independent kingdom and himself Richard Booth as its king. He even went as far as to declare his horse called Goldie as 'Prime Minister'. It's safe to say the man had a quirky sense of humour.

Booth was talented when it came to publicity and his stories and doings made the press. Disaster happened in 1977 when a fire broke out which brought the roof come down and destroyed many original features.

During the eighties the castle spent a lot of the time being a building site.

By 2000, the roof had been replaced and Booth had a bookstore open on the ground floor selling a mix of antique and second-hand books.

I have loved every castle I've visited, often each for different reasons, whether it be a ruin of distressed stone against a sweeping, rugged landscape, telling its story of battle, or of slighting and abandonment, often the perfect muse for moody photography, or a mix of both original and restored that invites you to step through time, into their world.

Of all the castles, I've mentioned previously, here's my top five and why:

Coming in at number five for architectural reasons is Raglan Castle.

After parking in the carpark and heading up the path, this castle's splendour hits you in the face, thanks to its magnificent gatehouse and striking turrets.

Perhaps the most impressive though is the great tower with its base surrounded by a filled in moat.

Another reason for this castle making my top five, is that its silhouette runs against the backdrop of the Monmouthshire countryside and offers picturesque views from its towers.

Coming in at number four is Caerphilly Castle. It looks like a peaceful sleeping giant, just waiting to be called back to the front lines.

Raglan Castle.

There are many reasons why I love this castle. I love that it appears to be a fearsome fortress floating effortlessly upon water. It's the perfect picturesque object for photography, another favourite pastime of mine.

I find it interesting that although this castle in Wales was built by an Englishman, it was the fear of a Welsh prince that inspired it.

I love the grandness of the great hall; its replicable weaponry in the grounds; but overall, if I am honest, I really wanted to visit Wales's version

A photograph taken from Wogans Cavern.

of its very own leaning tower, which did not disappoint. It appears as if it is held up by some invisible strings.

Coming in at number three is Pembroke Castle. There is plenty to see and explore.

For me to be able to stand in the birthplace of Henry VII. Who changed the course of history is remarkable.

My other favourite thing about this castle is what lies beneath. On the northern side under the castle is Wogan Cavern. This can be found down a long spiral staircase and is now home to horseshoe bats. It is a vast cave, and again feeds into my curiosity of who or what has gone before.

Artefacts found from here can be dated to the Roman period and some even to prehistoric times. Mammoth and reindeer bones have both been discovered in the cave, along with some tools that would have been left behind by early Homo sapiens. Excavations here are on-going.

Coming in at number two is Cardiff Castle, nestled in the heart of the city of Cardiff. I adore this castle as for a person like myself who loves history, it's almost as if you can walk through time whilst visiting. One minute you are looking at the red sandstone from the Roman period, then onto the Normans, to the Gothic splendour of the Butes, right through to the tunnels that protected the people of Cardiff during the Blitz.

Being looked after and restored, everywhere you turn Cardiff Castle offers you something else and openly invites you into its history and its many occupants.

For example, you can walk into the banqueting hall and feel like the Bute family will be shortly conducting a dinner party; or Lady Bute's bedroom where it seems she has just gone downstairs for her breakfast.

This castle is full of opulence and splendour with all its incredible extravagant interiors. It really is a wonder to see.

From the top of the castle, you are rewarded with epic views Cardiff.

As amazing as Cardiff Castle is, and as much as I have loved all the castles that I have visited, there is one that takes my top spot, one I fell in love with, one that is yet to be beaten for me and that is the splendour of Dinefwr.

Though I have to say that on my very first visit to Dinefwr, the day probably could not have gone any better in my eyes. If you recall my favourite season that I've previously mentioned, picture now a drizzly autumnal day and having had enough of being stuck in doors, you venture out on a quest to the ancient Kingdom of Deheubarth.

You arrive at the carpark and start the walk up the hillside.

On this day the already beautiful landscape was beginning to become full of the colours of autumn and on the ascent to the castle, the fallen leaves crunched beneath my feet, like a golden orange river leading the way to this romantic ruin.

Then walking through a patch of woodland, the castle was revealed.

On our arrival at the castle, it was ours alone to explore, probably due to being a cold rainy day. We climbed the spiral staircases, taking care as these can be slippery when it's been raining.

We then walked up the steps that took us to a top wall, and this was probably one of, if not the moment that sealed Dinefwr as a favourite.

We went looking for a view, though expected to see very little due to the weather. However, what we saw from the top of the castle was nothing short of magical.

From the cold stone, we looked out, the sky all clouded and foggy, and as the mist lifted from the ground, it revealed a luscious rich green landscape that went on as far as the eye could see.

In a sharp contrast to the stories of rebellions and conquests, there was calmness, a sea of rolling green and just the sound of nature herself.

On leaving the castle, we made our way down towards Newton House, which on our first visit was temporarily closed, but we still were able to walk around the grounds.

With this so far being my favourite place in Wales, of course I've been there more than once.

For me Dinefwr is a place that just keeps giving. On another visit with the weather being better, we were able to see the magnificent White Park Cattle in a field opposite Newton House. These creatures look almost mythical, and they have great historical and genetic relevance to Dinefwr. They are a rare and endangered breed that have roamed this area for over a thousand years.

We then visited the Grade II listed building of Newton House, which is a hub of history and a must for history lovers.

The exterior of the house boasts a Gothic style façade that was fashionable in the 1850s; a style I love seeing and photographing.

There are still some original features within the house including the fourteenth century grand staircase and ornate ceilings.

Cattle at Dinefwr.

On leaving the house, we walked through the 100-acre medieval deer park, another Dinefwr treat.

We then explored the landscape taking full advantage of the views.

Overall, for me Dinefwr is an amazing place to visit, it's like stepping into a fairy tale. You are transported away from the outside world and find yourself completely surrounded by rolling landscapes and structures that have seen generation after generation.

I will say that when I visit somewhere for the first time and begin a new obsession, I am prone to state 'this place is my favourite', however, so far it has always been rapidly followed by 'well, second to Dinefwr'.

Castles next on my wish list are all in the North of Wales: Caernarfon; Harlech; and Conwy.

Walking Welsh History: A History of South and Mid-Wales on Foot

An example of castle steps, my favourite kind.

CHAPTER FOUR

Kilvey Hill

Kilvey Hill is a large hill that dominates the South Wales city of Swansea. The hill can be glimpsed from many an area within the city and is a crucial part of Swansea's identity. It is steeped in its history and has many connections throughout the area and is known by probably everyone living in Swansea or Swansea-born.

It is an iconic part of the Swansea eastern side and has been a witness to the developments and changes within Swansea and also to the many generations that have lived in the area.

It has seen in its more recent times the dumping and burning of stolen or old cars that have been driven up on to the hill via Morris Lane, though authorities have been clamping down on this and barriers have been put in place to block cars.

Even today as I write this there is a considerable debate over Kilvey Hill with environmentalists wishing to protect the area and its species, and on the other side, a proposal to develop a £34,000,000 hilltop attraction. More on that later, first let's paint a picture of this splendiferous landscape and its history.

Today Kilvey Hill stands as a beautiful green place full of nature, with scenic walking routes and an amazing view of the city, but there is

A path that leads towards the top of Kilvey Hill.

much history that has come before, as this is not Kilvey Hill's original greenery.

There are a few different routes to access the hill, but probably the one used the most and my starting point is a free carpark at the bottom of the hill in the community woodland of Kilvey. This is a relatively small carpark. On the opposite side of the road slightly further up is Swansea park and ride, a much bigger carpark, however this would be a payable carpark.

From this entrance you walk underneath a wooden arch and start your ascent of the hill. You walk through trees of green leaves and hear the sounds of nature, and have beautiful views.

Although due to fir trees, the hill's panoramic splendour cannot be enjoyed in entirety from any one spot; it's worth moving around a bit to make the most of it.

The hill is also used by off-road bikers, sometimes unlicensed.

As to the history, the area of Kilvey from the 1100s was an eastern appendage of the Lordship of Gower.

It's not too difficult to picture what medieval Kilvey would have looked like; the landscape would have been very suitable for animals, growing food and clean streams would have been flowing. You just have to imagine farmlands.

However, this was not to be the Kilvey Hill that would remain.

The boom of the Industrial Revolution took off a lot quicker in Swansea than the rest of Wales due to its ready access to coal.

Swansea and Wales as a whole have had a long, intertwined relationship with coal. Kilvey's history can also be tightly linked to the adjoining White Rock and Middle Bank copperworks.

Kilvey and coal shared an intimate bond until the First World War. Mining took place here from as far back as Roman times, up until the mines on the hill were closed in the 1920s.

You can still spot signs, for example, through the waste tips with their strange shapes on the landscape, even though now overgrown, or the mine workings sometimes uncovered by badgers.

Since Kilvey's coal mining came to a halt many years ago, this rock that once dominated activity in the area for centuries is almost invisible to now see.

The early coal tips from before the start of the official recordings are often more difficult to locate as there is no fixed record or reference. The coal outcrops on the hill once of great importance are now buried beneath regrowth, landscaping, and deliberate attempts to hide them away.

There is no way of telling how much coal Kilvey produced due to so much being undocumented or just unknown.

With the population vastly increasing, so did the local use of coal.

Coal from Kilvey could have been used for exporting to other areas as well as for local use.

By the 1750s, coal was becoming a much more valuable commodity and so land containing coal increased in its value.

Coal was used for various things from fires to powering machinery and steam engines. There was a clear switch away from waterpower to steam power between the 1780s and the 1820s.

Today with the climate crisis being top of mind and the understanding of fossil fuels far greater, there is no doubt that a link can be made here back to the Industrial Revolution.

Moving away from waterpower had a big impact upon Kilvey as care for water resources was abandoned and instead huge waste tips appeared, which increased ecological damage that was already in place due to the smoke released when smelting copper ore.

Kilvey's coal history is lengthy although it is mainly undocumented, with much being passed down through words and practical experience.

With the addition of the White Rock Copperworks and other later industries, there was needed investment for coal exploration and this required knowledge of finances and extraction techniques.

For eighteenth-century industry to continue to grow, the tradition of coal mining on Kilvey and the surrounding areas needed to be fully understood and the proof of the existence of and the size of the coal resources, also had to be completely understood.

With the coal trade booming in the 1750s, it added new expenses such as those of steam technology.

There was an ever developing need to mine deeper and deeper and that meant that there had to be clear certainty that the mines were being dug in the right place.

Drift mines of Kilvey followed identifiable coal veins on the surface.

The many years of mining had led to people learning some facts regarding the coal that was being lifted from the ground. The coal's quality varied on where in the area it had been found. Also, the coal veins were interspersed with materials such as sandstones.

The Pennant sandstone of Swansea that swept through the cool veins was a building material often used for houses, canals and railways, before the cheap red bricks were available.

Another issue that came into play was faulting in the veins; some were cracked and broken with many faults which allowed for a coal vein to disappear from view in a tunnel and could continue for metres above or below the coalface.

Faulting could have impaired the viability of any of the coal mines. Coal mining continued to develop on Kilvey into the late eighteenth century while less productive sites were abandoned.

Kilvey Hill

The history of Kilvey can also be closely linked to copper, in particular to the White Rock Copperworks. Copper and Swansea also have a close-knit connection, and I will be tackling copper in my next chapter.

It is hard to envisage the copper smoke engulfing the Kilvey you can see today, but there are descriptions of black smoke and even times where breathing could be difficult. I can only imagine what wet weather would have caused. There would have been pollution and filth everywhere as opposed to the green and vibrant area we enjoy today.

Across the area, trees were becoming a distant memory, witnesses record oak, ash and sycamore trees being left as dead wood standing silently across Kilvey.

The pollution and smoke would have also had an effect on animals, that would have been made to graze and lay upon this toxic grass. This could have led these animals to suffer things such as deformities of their mouths, and possibly death.

Kilvey had become barren, the lush fields that grew potatoes and the corn bearing lands soon began to disappear.

By the 1800s, around half of the world's copper was being smelted in the lower Swansea Valley.

The copper-magnate Grenfell family in 1806 constructed terraced cottages across the lower slopes to house their many workers and their families.

The Grenfell's works employed around 800 people. The workers' families lived on the banks at Foxhole, Pentrechwyth and other places around the area of the hill.

In 1832, a number of farmers from the lower Swansea Valley took on a master of the copperworks in what is described as the Great Copper Trial. It was against John Henry Vivian and proved to be a very one-sided fight.

The farmers argued that the polluted smoke was causing severe harm to their cattle with their teeth becoming elongated and growing over each other. The horses were similar affected with their teeth blackening and decaying, all this ultimately preventing the animals from eating. Others testified that their cattle's bones were brittle and lumps were appearing on their knees and legs.

The farmers lost the case and industry carried on growing and ravaging for another 150 years.

Swansea was one of the world's earliest industrial areas.

But celebrating this industrial past does require artistic interpretation and imagination as many industrial structures have been demolished over the past century.

There's been a shift over the past few decades to restore Kilvey Hill to its former greener glory, and though it will never be fully what it was before the Industrial Revolution, there has been a big improvement environmentally.

The effort to climb this hill that stands guard over Swansea is rewarded when you stand at the top and you are greeted by panoramic views over the city and the docks.

There are stories of the past though that describe it as a 'wasteland hill', where children played in old abandoned mine workings and would return home with their knees blackened by carbon.

A photograph that I took of the view at the top of Kilvey Hill.

Kilvey Hill

If this hill could talk, it would be able to tell us amazing stories; it has seen everything from the first Iron Age forts to heavy industries and then bombing in the Second World War.

It is more than a nod to Swansea's industrial past, but also to when in the 1960s people came together to rebuild and bring back the greenery.

In the 1960s, Kilvey Hill was a playground for children; people tell stories of how they would slide down the built-up mineshafts on old milk crates.

Those kids would have been playing in a very toxic area.

Kilvey Hill even battled the Nazis when it withstood bombing after the Germans miscalculated the hill for the docks.

In 1954 a discovery of what was believed to be an Iron Age earthwork was uncovered on the northern side of Kilvey Hill.

A local historian called Bernard Morris carried out excavation works there in 1968. A sherd of a Samian bowl was unearthed at the site and a few stone cairns were found further up the hill although the date of their time period is unknown.

Kilvey Hill has been geographically in charge of Swansea since the city was founded. This is due to how it constricts the Tawe Valley, forcing roads and transport links to go around the hill via Llansamlet or towards the south around the area of Fabian Bay.

It is perhaps difficult to grasp the importance of coal today, because of the ever-increasing issue of climate change, but earlier generations would have heavily relied on it.

There would have been much talk of coal within the communities of Swansea. The locating of coal veins was important.

Coal working signs have made their mark on many a hillside in Swansea, from Afon Llan near Penllergaer across Townhill and the Eastern slopes of Kilvey Hill. Small quarries and outcrops show coal workings or explorations as people tried to find easy access to coal.

Swansea's long-time experience with coal meant that local knowledge of coal qualities and where it was available was incredible. This knowledge was crucial, and pooling this collective together was highly important.

There is a source from 1400 that can provide us with an insight into the early coal mining at Kilvey. In a group of accounts, showing the income for the Lordship of Gower, there is a report on the activities and income for an unnamed Kilvey coal mine over the period of a year. It is highly likely that the site in question was close to either White Rock or Foxhole as it would have had to have been near either the Hughes or the Foxhole coal vein.

It was a decent operation employing three miners and thirty porters who were tasked with bringing the coal from the mine in wheelbarrows, down to the riverside to be exported to Cornwall, Devon, Ireland and even France. Around 4,000 tonnes of coal was produced by the mine in 1400, though it is tough to say if this was a good amount for the time or not.

There was also a need for candles, repairs of tools, wheelbarrows and tubs to go under the ground on sledges in order to move the coal away from the workface.

A problem for them appears to have been water and to solve this issue, drainage and guttering was essential to help deal with the flows of the underground water.

This enterprise was a drift mine which followed the veins of coal via small tunnels cut into the sides of the hill. This type of drift mining was very suited to the geology of coal veins in Kilvey. The western side of the hill shows a lot of rock exposure and trenches that indicate extensive drift mining from 1300 to the 1750s.

Kilvey Hill had been subjected to early exploitation of its coal deposits, leading the hill to be scattered with over 700 years of coal workings.

With sophistication growing, the mining industry commanded higher productive coal pits in the 1700s.

With westerly winds a lot of the pollution from the lower valley dispersed over Kilvey, both ruining land in the area and destroying the ecosystem.

From 1970, the environmental condition of Kilvey has steadily recovered to what we can see today.

Kilvey Hill's importance to Swansea's environmental history is seen in how the lower Swansea Valley industries both exploited and destroyed the land in an ecological sense.

Industrialisation continues to have implications and shape the local landscape and geography for both the present and the future. Kilvey stood as an example of how horrific pollution could be, and as an example of the lack of care from the local industrialists.

Though on the other side of the same coin, Kilvey also stands as a focus of restoration and repair, even if that was picked up by the public sector, when the private industrialists deserted their responsibilities during the Great Depression.

Restoring greenery to the hill has been nothing but remarkable, when you think of the lifeless toxic wasteland it once was in the 1940s.

As I write this, Kilvey Hill stands as the last remaining undeveloped hill of Swansea Bay, but as mentioned earlier, there is a lot of controversy regarding Kilvey Hill due to the proposed huge leisure development, including a skyline cable car and luge.

Some people fear this will eat into the countryside and the nature of the hill, while others have argued that it is moving with the times and will bring more tourists and money into the area.

Will all the effort to regreen the area have been in vain if the skyline is installed?

It is with a New Zealand-based company called Skyline Enterprises, who have promised to still keep access to the hill, but of course with some safety restrictions.

They have said the proposed cable lift will enable more people to have access to the hill and its stunning views. This cable car system would run from beneath the hill from the Hafod and Morfa Copperworks area.

There is also talk of a swing, a zip line, adding to the existing walking trails and added mountain bike paths.

It is said to be a boost for jobs in the area and is a multi-million-pound investment.

It is one of the biggest single investments in tourism and hospitality that Wales has seen in recent years. There will also be beverage outlets near the top of the hill.

Swansea would become the first place within the United Kingdom and indeed Europe to join such places like New Zealand as a skyline destination, if this proposal was to go ahead.

There is much opposition from locals in the area who worry this is damaging for the environment and the way people have fought for decades to bring greenery back to Kilvey Hill.

Which side are you on?

Trees on Kilvey Hill.

CHAPTER FIVE

Swansea and Copper

Swansea and copper have a deep-rooted connection, their Welsh histories are intertwined, and copper is a major part of the city's history.

It all started at the beginning of the eighteenth century. Swansea was to become the place with the new revolutionary method of smelting copper that would later become known as the Welsh Process. Using coal as its source of energy, the Swansea smelters were allowed to manufacture copper in huge volumes and Swansea went on to become a smelting centre of great importance within Europe. Swansea was producing a third of the world's melted copper and sometimes even more than this.

What made the Welsh Process so effective was that the ore was brought to the fuel, instead of the other way around. Coal was the source of the change in technology here, but organisational and special arrangements were also needed and important. The main source in Britain for copper ore in the eighteenth century was Cornwall. Due to the Cornish mines being so close to the coast, the ore could be sent straight across the Bristol Channel to Swansea.

A co-dependency developed between Cornwall and Swansea. In return for the ore, Swansea sent back Welsh coal in order to power the Cornish steam engines that worked in the mines. That was until the 1770s when there

A close-up of chimneys that remain a nod to Swansea's industrial past.

was an exploitation of ore on the island of Anglesey off the coast of North Wales. Parys Mountain ores could be extracted by open cut methodology which gave them a big advantage over the deep mined products in England.

There was a crisis for Cornwall. But the Anglesey deposits were exhausted within a generation and Cornwall once again would become dominant in the early years of the nineteenth century and would not be challenged again until the 1830s. A relaxation in the British regulation system at the end of the 1820s meant that the supply chain could get bigger. Ore once restricted to British and Irish waters was now able to leave for further distant harbours. Welsh copper seemed to be in a position of no limits; it received orders from places such as Cuba, Colombia, Peru and Chile. With this growth, early Victorian Swansea became so much more than an industrial hub: it had become 'Copperopolis', a term that is greatly used by historians today to describe the time.

Cornish miners were sent to Cuba; railway engineers to Chile; and those in the know about smelting set sail for Adelaide, Australia. With this carefully organized network to far off places, Swansea's copper helped Britain's Industrial Revolution go global. However, the very success of Swansea became problematic when the Welsh Process started to make reckless use of coal.

As advances in fuel efficiency emerged, the Welsh Process began to shift away from its reliance on the coal-rich regions of Swansea and South Wales. Investments in the railroad led to a shake up in the geography of the nineteenth century copper production as it offered a number of options. The Swansea centre role would now move away to a more polycentric style.

The American copper industry tried to follow the Welsh pattern, but they quickly grew much bigger and before the nineteenth century was over, they had adopted methods that varied from this Swansea Welsh method.

In the 1860s, Swansea's global dominance drew to an end, but it did remain an important smelting district for decades into the future. Its output of smelted copper did not even peak until the 1890s, but global production reduced rapidly in the final part of the nineteenth century.

Swansea's part was becoming one of a more specialized processing and refining roll. Smelting ore finally ceased in the latter part of the twentieth century; overgrown and weathered ruins with acres of slag waste were all that remained.

So that was an introduction to Swansea and its copper history to paint a picture of where you could be walking around, but let's delve deeper back to the very beginning and how it came about and who was involved.

Let's start with the Llangyfelach operation, headed up by Dr John Lane and John Paul Pollard. Having relocated their enterprise to Swansea after failing at Neath Abbey in 1716, a move of about six miles, it was the spark for a new beginning as it was the first copperworks to be established in what would become a town of major copper operation.

Reasons why the men quit Neath is a difficult question, perhaps it was for the benefits that Swansea brought being bigger and with easier access to the sea and a decent harbour. Within Swansea, coal deposits could be found abundantly. Swansea town was also able to benefit from less gentry influence, partly thanks to the main landowner, the Duke of Beaufort, being just an occasional visitor. Beaufort's interests were taken care of by local agents, who had a favourable opinion towards industrial enterprises upon the duke's land.

The men from Neath set up their new industrial venture at Landore, about two miles up the river from Swansea harbour, leasing their site from a local landowner Thomas Popkin. It can sometimes be referred to as the Llangyfelach Copperworks, as that was the name taken by some contemporaries because of the parish in which the works were situated. Lane and his partners were expertly equipped with the latest technology, and they hoped to operate on a larger scale than any of the smelting works that came before in Bristol. By 1727, the works had grown to a labour force of forty men and two boys; people such as Rhys Morgan Harry and Evan Jenkin were among the workforce and the prevalence of the Welsh names is highly suggestive that they were either Swansea locals or that they had been brought along from Neath. The works itself consisted of twenty smelting furnaces, a refining house, a forge and a mill for copper rod. It came in at around a sum of £2,000 to build.

Just four years later, a second copper smelting enterprise appeared in Swansea, this was called the Cambrian Copperworks, and it was constructed south of Lane's work on the land that unsurprisingly belonged to the Duke of Beaufort. Two of the duke's agents were behind this development: Gabriel Powell Sr and a rent collector named Silvanus Bevan.

Bevan was a Swansea Quaker with his presence known in the business communities of both Swansea and the brass industry of Bristol in the early eighteenth century, which could have been the reason behind using the services of another Quaker, James Griffiths, to run this new enterprise at the Cambrian Copperworks. Even with two copper smelting works in a very favourable position not far from Swansea's large harbour where there was an easy transport line straight to the furnace, it was not completely perfect nor plain sailing. The early years of these operations were marked by the 1720 financial crisis which brought collapse in the share prices in the East India Company, South Sea Company and the Royal African Company.

John Lane himself was in financial uncertainty, and he was bankrupted in the 1720s. His enterprise became under the management and control of his previous assistant, Robert Morris. If Lane was a co-founder of copper smelting in Swansea, then Morris would secure the Llangyfelach works operations and would go on to establish their location as profitable and thus making it more attractive to investors, such as Humphrey Mackworth.

The works would face yet another crisis as soon as 1727 when a fever outbreak infected William Bevan and six other copper men, resulting in the death of a worker named Jenkin Johns.

Setbacks like these were part and parcel of the uncertain environment that these early entrepreneurs of Swansea were working in. The Cambrian works most likely faced similar issues. At this point, there was not a clear picture that copper smelting had a secure future at this site or that both businesses were indeed sustainable in the area.

Morris seems to have been able to survive the early knocks, the fate of Griffiths is unclear, but we do know that by 1735 Morris had taken over the Cambrian works and later these works would be converted into a pottery-making premises.

Perhaps Morris' success came from his willingness to immerse himself within his business, extending a level of personal control over it, extending to wages and employee structures.

Key furnacemen and refiners' services were highly sought after and, in a bid to secure them, Morris drew up a range of strict agreements with his employees. Those workers that were trained in the latest methods were given contracts of either three or four years and sometimes they would have to give a twelve-month notice period. To Bevan, Morris paid an annual income of £80, add to this the value of items such as candles and coal and his earnings were actually around the £100-mark. Most workers were paid weekly, with refiners getting about twelve shillings.

Morris also looked into the source of fuel supplies. Under his lease of the works, he had to purchase his coal from his landlord, Thomas Popkin, who owned nearby mines. This arrangement seems to have worked well under

Dr Lane, but under the control of Morris and in the later 1720s, the smelting activity had stepped up a notch and more coal was needed more often. In just a three-month time scale in the latter half of 1728, around eighteen 'weys' of coal per week was being devoured by Morris's enterprise and Popkin could not meet his growing demand, only able to supply less than a quarter of the requirement.

As was custom, Popkin also sold his coal to clients in the West Country, Ireland and even as far as France. Morris suspected that the coal reserve being kept for him was of the poorest quality for smelting works. As a result, from the 1730s Morris started to investigate taking more control of the supply of coal by taking shares in his own collieries. He was to join forces with a man named Walter Hughes and his very trusted associate from Bristol John Padmore to mine at Llanrhidian to the west of Swansea on the Gower Peninsula. This brought about a reliable source for his fuel for his works and also he was able to sell any excess. He also made sure he had access to various suppliers.

A small number of copper mines in America produced for export in the early eighteenth century as it was prohibited for colonies to smelt. An important supplement to the Cornish ore was Barbary copper from the north of Africa. This all would go on to play a crucial role as the accounts of Morris' operation in Llangyfelach for the latter 1720s and early 1730s show Barbary copper to have had a big share of the copper produced here.

By the third decade in the eighteenth century with Barbary copper purchases high, a few London merchants, including Morris's chief investor Richard Lockwood, petitioned the government asking for a lift of the duty that was imposed on its import. Lockwood's investment helped to fund the first big expansion since Morris's takeover of the business. A new water-powered battery mill was constructed upriver from the Llangyfelach works in upper forest. Copperware such as plates, bowls and other goods were a staple of the copperworks

In 1728 John Padmore, a Bristol engineer, was brought in to help Morris view potential sites along the River Tawe for his mill. Padmore had expertise in how waterpower could be harnessed. The mill was built and was working by 1731 upon land that was sourced and secured from the Duke of Beaufort.

There was a transformation that happened for Swansea's copper in the mid-eighteenth century. There was a bigger demand now for copper processing vessels in the Caribbean sugar division and also for goods such as manillas and Guinea rods.

Manillas were horseshoe shaped small items, cast in brass or copper lead alloy which became popular as a use of currency and as ornamental wear. These items were produced in Swansea copperworks from the 1720s.

Guinea rods were small lengths of copper sold on the West African coast around the mid-eighteenth century. Like manillas, they were being sold to those involved in the slave trade. Guinea rods were sometimes carried as part of the cargo that in turn would be exchanged for slaves.

With Morris's early successes, it led his rival smelters to rethink the location of their own businesses. The first sign of this was in 1731 when Thomas Coster and Co made the first step towards relocating its works to the Swansea district.

Coster had taken over the Melincryddan works in Neath as Humphrey Mackworth passed away in 1727, leaving behind a son in a lot of debt. By letting go of the copperworks, he was able to concentrate his efforts on coal mining interests. Coster indeed smelted copper at Neath, but up until 1742, it had been more of a stepping stone towards getting closer to Morris' territory of the Swansea district. Coster, along with two Bristol merchants Joseph and Samuel Percival, signed a lease with the landowner Bussy Mansell for a part of the land at White Rock in Swansea. There was a commitment to building a new smelting house and around twenty furnaces within three years. It was clear that these new arrivals to the Swansea district understood that coal was key to their success, and they would be supplied by the landowner Mansell from his own collieries. With the knowledge that the Welsh-based smelters suspected that the best coal was not given to them, but sold elsewhere, Coster and Percival brought in quality control by suggesting that the coal should be subject to the refiners' approval.

Even though there was scope to develop here, in both smelting and processing, they chose to concentrate on the coal intensive smelting. At White Rock there was a narrow and long hall that was called the great workhouse, built to hold the smelting furnaces. Later a calcining house was constructed.

A photograph of some of the ruins of the Whiterock Copperworks Swansea.

By the middle of the century, it had grown and become a force in the copper smelting world. Its figures were comparing well with those of Morris and Lockwood. These two firms now stood tall on opposite sides of the River Tawe and Swansea started to see the effects. The town's population increased, being above 2,000 for the first time since the 1720s, due to a natural increase as well as immigration.

The harbour was busy due to there being about sixteen collieries in working order. Though the town of Swansea was developing, it still suffered from poor roads, had only two postal deliveries a week and anything resembling a bank facility did not exist yet.

Swansea had moved to the centre of British copper smelting operations over a space of just sixty years. At this point, it was still far from its full industrial potential and it was to grow and expand even further. By the early years of the nineteenth century, there was more and more of a demand for copper products, things like sheathing to protect ships' hulls, including

Swansea and Copper

A photograph of the river Tawe in Swansea. You can see some of the remains of a once bustling industry that swamped this area.

merchant and naval fleets; distilling operations; and boilers to be used in steam engines.

Over time, the banks of the River Tawe began to become overcrowded with new copper smelting works. The pre-existing premises of Llangyfelach and White Rock were joined by Middle Bank, Upper Bank, Rose, Ynys, Hafod and Morfa. Although the impact would be a double-edged sword, in the 1820s there were clear signs of new wealth beginning to improve the town and its facilities. However, on the other hand, smoke pollution of the lower Swansea Valley became a subject for debate.

Swansea's ascendancy was not linear in its progression as smelters had to battle the effects of conflicts in the political world, technology and competition for overseas produce. They required vigilance to be flexible and skilled in technology so they could withstand the quality demands of customers and keep at bay their rival competitors at home and abroad.

Middle Bank opened in 1755 and just two years later, Upper Bank was up and running, both on the east bank of the Tawe, north of White Rock.

The investors in these new works were Chauncy Townsend, a London merchant, and his son-in-law John Smith, a solicitor to the East India Company which provided him with knowledge to sell products in Asia. Townsend was both creative and ambitious, revealed in the fact that the furnace halls at Middle Bank were ten times bigger than the original works. He also had a copper mill at Wraysbury in Buckinghamshire with links to the London market. He even mined his own source of coal from Llansamlet and Landore and built a wooden tramway to transport the fuel down to the quarry.

Townsend and Smith made investments at Middle and Upper Bank and new investments also happened at the old original sites. By 1752, Lockwood, Morris and Co had relocated from their original site to be closer to their waterpower mill constructed two decades before. From here they had room to expand their rolling mill capacity. Growth was also seen at the White Rock site involving a number of Bristol-based partnerships that supplied copper to the mills in the city hinterland for processing. Joseph Percival, one of the original partners at White Rock in the 1730s, operated the works under his actual name up until 1764 from here it was taken over by John Freeman, another Bristol entrepreneur. Under Freeman, White Rock's production expanded vastly. These new expansions and extensions led to a steep rise in output.

Bristol in the 1740s and 1750 remained an important player in copper production, however by the outbreak of the American Revolution its brass and copper was in decline. In contrast, Swansea's operations were booming. However, while the smelting of ore was centred in South Wales, the actual processing of copper was not happening there. Even with the construction of battery works and rolling mills in the lower Swansea Valley, the copper produced here had to be sent elsewhere to be turned into sheets, rods and wire. Part was being processed in Bristol mills, but a large percentage was handled in London.

With the Swansea district gaining capacity as a copper smelting centre between 1750s and 1760s and becoming attractive to investors, there were also two new developments within the British copper trade that sped up the pace for change over the next couple of decades. One was the discovery of a good source of copper ore in Anglesey and the other, entering the maritime market with protective covering on ships' hulls.

Ticketing was still happening and the agents that companies would send here, were not only interested with getting a good purchase, but also quite sneakily some might say gathering business intelligence on other sites. Thomas Brown was an agent for Williams and Grenfell at the Upper Bank Copperworks and would often return from ticketing with the news and gossip of what was going on at rival companies.

John Vivian first went into the copper smelting industry in works in North Gower before constructing his own site at Hafod, situated along the West Bank of the River Tawe in 1809; whilst Pascoe Grenfell of Penzance and Owen Williams, son of Thomas Williams, came together in partnership that took over the Middle and Upper Bank Works in 1804. Grenfell had a background in banking and in dealing with copper and tin ore. He had been associated with Thomas Williams by acting as agent for him and after his passing in 1802, Grenfell continued at Swansea in partnership with Thomas' son.

From what remains in records we are able to have a few insights into both operations in the early nineteenth century. Williams and Grenfell seem to have been known as the leading copper smelting works in Britain as within the first ten years of the nineteenth century it topped the lists of copper ore purchases by large quantities.

They had two big smelting works in Swansea along with the mill in Buckinghamshire and Flintshire and in Liverpool they had a warehouse facility. The works were in a good position to be able to produce manufactured copper goods for both exporting and for home use. Reports from the Upper Bank Works over fortnightly periods from June to December 1829 tell us that just over 200 tonnes of ore was being smelted at these works. They used about fifteen furnaces and employed around forty-nine people.

Vivian had already been involved in the industry, though some described him as a latecomer, when he built his own smelting works in the lower Swansea Valley in 1808-09. The Vivian Hafod site, on the western bank of the Tawe, was almost directly opposite the Middle Bank operation. The Hafod works started out as a big smelting hall with twenty-four furnaces driven by coal that was delivered via an adjacent canal dock. Vivian's son, John Henry, oversaw production while Vivian secured the sales. But Hafod's production of copper cake was not going to be enough to sustain it as a profitable business, so the Vivians were prompted, probably by the demand for sheathing, to heavily invest in a mill facility equipped with steam-powered rolling equipment, so they could process copper into flat thin sheets that were in demand by shipbuilders and repairers. Without doing this, there would not have been any guarantee of securing a share of this new market.

The plans to construct this mill were quickly drawn up and it became operational by 1819. They also opened a nail manufacturing facility, making metal nails and spikes as well as some brass parts used for engines. By 1822, Vivian had also taken charge of the Forest Mills lease, works that had previously been developed under the management of Morris and Lockwood and were located around two miles upriver from the Vivian Hafod works. While the Hafod works did have warehouse space where they could temporarily store produce from the mill, there was a need for a facility that was nearer the main copper markets. By 1811 a London agent had been appointed by Thompson and Co as they were able to provide the Vivians with the warehouse and to build up their customer base.

The British Navy had been an important customer in the 1790s, but they had opened their own metal mills in the early nineteenth century and though wartime conditions did stimulate demand for domestic items, warfare also could have potentially disrupted the exports. After England's war against France in 1793, the shipments of copper sheathing and fastenings from America became less of a reliable source due to US ships trading with Britain being seized by French privateers.

American entrepreneur Paul Revere was part of a government incentive to learn the techniques of copper rolling and drawing. He was successful and was able to supply the navy with copper sheathing by 1803.

Vivian and sons felt the effect of this back in Swansea. In 1813 they were suffering the loss of the American market. The copper from overseas was not the only issue facing works who had invested in copper rolling manufacturing of sheeting and in the 1820s concerns were voiced by customers, including naval ones, about the durability of copper sheathing along with its huge price. Some reported needing to replace sheathing in less than five years.

Wishing to avoid the repeated expenses of regular refitting, the navy board went to the council of the Royal Society and officers of the Royal Mint to help with finding a more durable alternative to copper sheathing. Experiments took place to find materials cheaper, but tougher. Humphry

Davy found that introducing metals like zinc and iron could make the copper sheathing durable for longer and Robert Mushet found an alloy of copper together with zinc and tin lead to be more durable. Experiments were also taking place inside the copperworks with the Vivians turning the Forest Mills over to the rolling of sheets from copper regulus so that this may help them to be more durable. They followed the English patent for bronze sheathing that had been originally developed in France at the same time. Pascoe Grenfell had opted for the sheathing from yellow metal that had been developed by George Frederick Muntz. A cheaper option to copper, this ultimately won the navy's favour after of course being subjected to trials. In the end this search was taken over by shipbuilding developments and iron-hulled ships, but the experiments are evidence of just how adaptable and responsive the smelters had to be towards the ever-changing environment.

Copper was in demand in the beer brewing industry which had increased in the late eighteenth and early nineteenth centuries, particularly in Ireland after legislation was passed that encouraged consuming beer over that of whiskey.

Vivian and Sons by 1822 had gained a contract to supply thirty tonnes of copper monthly to London-based firm Shears and Co. which supplied copper vessels to the brewing industry. The firm had their own mills where vessels could be manufactured, and smaller quantities were supplied directly to brewers in the form of big copper bottoms with raised sides. One Irish customer called O'Connor placed an order with the Vivians for copper bottoms that were about eight feet in diameter with raised sides as well as a flat circle of copper that would form the closing dome of the brewing pan. The copper stock at Williams and Grenfell's warehouse is evidence that they were also producing similar items at the time.

Asia was the dominant market for the production of copper goods of which the East India Company was dominating and controlling the purchases and sales. They purchased 15,000 tonnes of copper annually for the Asia market and the Swansea works' anticipated sales amounted to a large piece of their yearly output. Securing an East India Company order was very probably a Swansea copper firm's target for the year. If awarded a contract, they had to deliver on their agreed terms so companies would tend to plan their other work around what they had committed to the Indian company.

Swansea copper went through a radical change towards the end of the 1820s.

The use of ores from further afield had not been an option due to the tariff barriers that had been in place. However, reforms were made in the 1820s that were intended to address this.

The ministers realized that Britain's dominance in the industrial world would be better served by the removal of export duties and the shift of any obstacles on imports of the raw materials. The lead on this was taken by the President of the Board of Trade, William Huskisson. His reforms of 1825 brought about a cut in the duty that was paid on imported ore, although this was not a full solution as duty was still high.

Two years later, the 1827 Customs Act brought in a crucial change in that copper ore could now be imported freely on condition that the metal made from it was exported. Swansea's smelters naturally jumped at the chance and with that, a global market opened up.

Ore was received from a number of places such as Mexico, Colombia, Chile and New Zealand among others. Along with these new shipments of ore, came key technologies, such as steam power to drain mines, and it also brought the immigration of skilled workers.

Swansea was now at the heart of things and was therefore instrumental in the globalization of the British Industrial Revolution. Along with these new developments came great responsibility, as Swansea now had an important role in Britain's commercial empire in the 1830s to 1840s.

When the 1827 Customs Act was brought in, the Swansea smelters first turned towards Latin America. They had good reasons for doing so.

After the wars brought independence, the newly formed republics were on the lookout for foreign investors. British capitalists were also keen to have access to markets in the former Spanish empire.

However, a lot of the mining companies neither had the local knowledge or the technical skills and relied on the London Exchange.

This led to a collapse of the boom and was most likely enough to deter a number of Swansea investors.

Richard Hussey Vivian of the Hafod Works was aware of the risks and compared it to walking in the dark.

Some of the Vivians who had close ties to the Cornish mining trade had worries that this new material could lead to consequences for them.

Others were less concerned, and some serious investors were tempted back by the wealth of Latin American resources.

Charles Pascoe Grenfell who was soon to be at the top of Pascoe Grenfell and Sons, of the Middle Bank operations, had shares in silver mines in Mexico and Gran Colombia. He also had a share of the Bolivar Mining Association, which included a copper mine.

Towards the end of the 1820s, derelict mines in the Sierra behind Santiago de Cuba became known to a British merchant called John Hardy Jr, who had settled there, attracted by the economic buoyancy due to the Haitian Revolution and the wars of liberation.

The area had become full of refugees, French planters and Spanish Royalists who had been attracted to Santiago de Cuba, bringing with them any wealth and slaves that they could take from the territories they were fleeing.

In February 1830, a partnership headed by John Hardy Jr, received a grant of the old mines from Cuba's Captain General. The new owners were a mix of Britons and well-connected locals. They set about restoring the mine to full working order. But it was a huge task and at first their progress was slow; if this site was going to be a big player on the world market, they would need an investment on a bigger scale than they already had.

By 1835, it was absorbed into a partnership that was dominated by financial and industrial personalities in Britain. The new company represented the incorporation of Cuban mines with that of the Welsh copper industry.

The first man to be chairman of this new company was Charles Pascoe Grenfell. His board of directors included Riversdale William Grenfell, Charles's half-brother and business partner from Pascoe Grenfell and Sons.

Not everyone who was associated with this rebirth had close ties to the Swansea district, but the ones who did not have a background in copper brought along a different set of expertise, mainly of a maritime nature.

The transportation of ore was now required across vast distances of ocean, a big leap when compared to the usual Bristol Channel.

The El Cobre company had been divided into 12,000 shares; Charles Pascoe Grenfell and his directors held 4,500 of these and the remaining shares were offered up to the public for a sale of £40 per share.

The operation at El Cobre could now become streamlined with technical advances. Naturally this was not to remain unnoticed; other investors became worried and wanted to exploit the mineral wealth at El Cobre.

By 1826 another company had acquired a grant of mineral property near to El Cobre's workings. The Royal Santiago Mining Company had in a similar fashion come together out of wealthy financiers, industrialists and people involved in shipping.

Just like before, this company also had Swansea links, particularly that of Michael Williams who was part of the consortium that had taken over at the Rose Copperworks in Swansea in 1823, along with his father and his brothers. They renamed themselves Williams Foster & Co and they constructed a new smelting operation in early 1830 at Morfa, just across the River Tawe from the Grenfell Middle Bank works.

Possibly this new sizeable venture at Morfa, combined with new works in the Neath Valley, led to Williams investing in Cuba to secure good ore supplies.

The large amounts that were raised for deployment in Cuba were needed to bring the technological quality that was required for them to be effective in the international markets.

Capital and skills would have been provided by Britain, while the unskilled labour force that would have numbered into the hundreds, would have been sourced locally. The specialist equipment and skilled labour force would have come from Cornwall.

Both of the new companies had some Cornish connections that they could exploit.

The family of Charles Pascoe Grenfell was from a tin mining parish of St. Just, in Cornwall's far west and Michael Williams was born near Redruth, in the county's central mining belt. So, Cornwall would have been a familiar location and territory to the key directors from both of the companies.

Though everything would not all be plain sailing as a tropical disease depleted the Cornish workforce. This illness was yellow fever, and it was having a devastating impact.

El Cobre was becoming more of a charnel house and this led to the lure quickly fading.

Swansea and Copper

By the beginning of the 1840s, the mining companies were being made to look further than Cornwall. With so many of the mine proprietors having interests in Wales, it offered itself as an alternative.

A man called William Thompson in the Santiago company took the lead, he was an owner of the Penydarren Iron Works in Merthyr Tydfil, along with being a city financier.

Workers began leaving Wales for Cuba, where indigenous miners were cheaper than their Cornish counterparts but lacked hard rock experience, which was often pointed out by the captains who were in charge of them. Even with a steady influx, workers who were European were in a minority at El Cobre.

The Cornish specialists were supported by a number of free descendants of African slaves who had worked in the mines in the seventeenth century.

Alongside the eighty British specialists, were around 150 Cuban or Spanish free workers along with 422 slaves. This was not unusual for nineteenth century Cuba, which due to a sugar boom saw African slaves brought in by their thousands despite the practice being outlawed in 1817 by an Anglo-Spanish treaty.

With there being a high demand for sugar, the inflow of African slaves continued unabated through clandestine channels although the enslavers did not try to disguise their activities. So violating was this contraband trade that the British pushed a new treaty on the Spanish in 1835. This had little effect however, and around 108,000 slaves landed in Cuba in the latter part of the 1830s; many of them were sent to the cane fields, but a few of them were destined for a different role – underground labour for Santiago de Cuba.

There was no advertising of the use of slave labour by the mining companies as abolitionists were very active in Britain in the mid-1830s. In 1834, slavery had been abolished in Britain's Caribbean possessions. The 1835 Spanish treaty gave a new force for Britain's mission against the slave trade.

Understandably, it would be a big embarrassment if any British mining companies were to be identified as slave owners and traders. Rumours around what was happening had made their way to the Foreign Office, leading the British consul in Santiago to investigate.

The British consul was John Hardy Jr, who was faced with delving into his own wicked actions and activities. Hardy tried to put a positive spin on the Cobre company's large number of slaves, claiming this had been forced on the company due to there not being enough workers from the free population and that these were longstanding slaves who had offered themselves for purchase due to being dissatisfied with their current master. However, this explanation convinced no-one.

Diary entries by James Whitburn, a Cornish engineman, painted a very different picture as he speaks of the cruelty to which slaves were subjected. He speaks of violence being inflicted upon the enslaved people, and that in El Cobre mines this kind of violence was part of the routine. Beatings happened daily.

In 1841 the Cuban census showed slavery was fundamental to copper mining at El Cobre. This scandal could not go on being disguised forever. By 1841 the slave holding companies had been brought to the attention of anti-slavery groups in Britain.

The British and Foreign Anti-Slavery Society started a campaign against the continuing involvement of British people in Atlantic slavery, and attention was paid to the various mining companies. There was the introduction of a parliamentary bill that would prohibit the practice of using slaves in the mining sector. The British would now be blocked from making use of slave labour anywhere in the world regardless of the local laws.

Companies including those of Cobre and Santiago lobbied against this, and did manage to gain two concessions: they did not have to free the slaves that were already owned, although the companies could not purchase any new slaves; and they were able to hire slaves from other owners.

This was not the result abolitionists had hoped for.

In the 1840s the ore that was dominating the British market was Cuban; this was due to the mines being controlled directly by British companies. They had used Cornish technology, slaves and capital that could drive up output rapidly.

But in Chile things were arranged in a different manner, though it was an important source for the British smelters in the 1830s and 1840s. A big difference was that British involvement in mining here was an exception and not the norm. There was not a load of Cornish technology here nor did slaves make up the fundamental force of mining labour.

It was after their independence that copper production had started to grow.

Whilst they had been under Spanish rule, Chilean copper was shipped to Peru and to other parts of Spain's American empire. Chilean ports now were able to open up to foreign shipping, including direct export to India, that was overseen by British-run merchant houses in Calcutta.

These ports started to grow and develop.

At this point, exports from Chile were in a smelted form and not in ore. Copper could only be transported for export in smelted form up until 1834.

After the shipment of ore was authorized, it was clear there was a regional divide between central and northern Chile. The traditional smelting districts in Valparaiso continued to export in the form of bars; ore shipments did happen here, but not to any great level. In the provinces of Copiapo and Huasco, it was a different story.

Firewood was difficult to come by in the northern parts and this new rapid pace quickly put added strain on its supplies.

Local smelters were at a disadvantage so shipping abroad was their better option. The export numbers showed a steep increase, which was mirrored in the figures for ore imports to Britain.

In the early 1830s, Chilean ore started appearing on the British market, but in an experimental way.

Then there was an upward surge in imports from 1,670 tons in 1834 to 3,812 tons in 1835, and then another leap in 1836 to 8,693 tons. By this point, Chilean ore was matching and sometimes surpassing Cuban ore in the British markets.

The products available to the Swansea district had been vastly extended by the introduction of Cuban and South American copper ores.

In 1840, Swansea was well and truly cemented as the central smelter.

The ore that had previously been restricted to British waters, now found its way around the Chilean headland and soon they would find their way to make port in Australia providing the Swansea copper companies with an unprecedented reach.

The 1840s saw the Swansea district at its fullest. There were three works to the far west, on lands bordering the Loughor Estuary; they were the Llanelly Copperworks; Cambrian Copperworks; and the Spitty Bank Works, although the lower Swansea Valley contained the highest concentration of smelting operations, with nine operating in 1840. They were all near to Swansea's coal seam and its supplies.

On one side of the river stood White Rock, Middle Bank and Upper Bank; and on the other side the Hafod, Morfa, Landore, Rose, Birmingham and Forest Works.

The Swansea Valley was also, and probably rightly so, the location of the largest works, these being Morfa and Hafod.

The Neath Valley was home to Mines Royal Co and Crown Cooper Co.

The Afan Valley formed the eastern boundary of the Swansea district with the Margam Works having been built during the American Revolutionary War and at the beginning of the 1840s, it was being run by the Vivians.

On the other hand, the works at Cwmavon was a new upstart by English Copper Co.

In whichever copperworks workers found themselves, it would have been very demanding. They would have been fed well, clothed and housed adequately, but they also would have been subjected to lots of heat and smoke. Undoubtedly safety standards were not as we know them today; for example, a furnaceman's clothing would not have offered him much

This photograph depicts remnants of the Copper Works of Swansea, located on the Hafod-Landore side of the river Tawe.

protection at all. In an attempt to protect themselves against the toxic gases, workers most likely had only their neckerchiefs to rely on, using them to cover their noses and mouths.

Also, they would have been frequently subjected to sulphuric acid because when ore was taken from the calcining furnaces, it was not fully desulfurized and therefore would expel clouds of sulphurous gases and sulphuric acids.

Both these are extremely corrosive and would have contaminated a worker's throat and nose.

Sulphuric acid was difficult to disperse due to it being a heavier substance than air. This was even more damaging for the worker and could leave them with red and cracked skin and could even attack dental enamel if the concentration levels were high enough.

Arsenic emissions would also have been a concern and damaging environmentally.

Nearby farmers would find their crop fields began to fail and their animals sickened, many dying.

The value of their land would also take a hit as an effect.

As a result, copper companies ended up being at the heart of legal disputes.

In 1820, the Vivians were accused of being a common nuisance by the High Sheriff of Glamorgan, who was also a landowner in the Tawe Valley. This did go to trial, but following indictments, didn't make it into a courtroom.

The copper masters hired some of the best people around to plead their case, both lawyers and scientists. Judges were ruling in favour of the copperworks. One defence was that by building stacks of great height, they were able to disperse the smoke away safely.

The workers suffered from chronic illnesses and in 1843 a furnacemen's strike took place as they claimed that they were losing two to three months of the year to illness. Their employers had anticipated this and had substitutes ready to step in for those furnacemen not fit to work. In 1843 at the Hafod Works around thirty-six substitutes were on standby.

Workers were also excluded from any benefit society.

With the London *Morning Chronicle* in the early 1850s claiming that wages were good, strikes were rare, and sons would often succeed their fathers at the copperworks.

The truth of the claim is unclear as the Swansea district's formative years are poorly recorded with regards to labour. The writings of Frederic Le Play provide us with an insight into the history of work in Swansea's copper operations. He was a professor at the Ecole des Mines, where the elite of promising engineers in France undertook their training. He visited Swansea for the first time in 1836, followed by two further trips and a publication in 1848 consisting of nearly 500 pages and an analysis of the Welsh Process.

In his book he paid attention to the workforce, where many others had just concentrated on the smelting of the copper. Le Play saw the worker as an important part of the process and understanding how men and women interacted to improve the technology was his approach.

For example, he noted what weights the workers had to lift, the distances they needed to walk and any incline they needed to ascend. He also placed an importance on the family unit, the lifecycle of his subjects. He therefore can provide an unrivalled guide to the ways youngsters were inducted into the copperworks and what roles they could undertake.

A reverberatory furnace was worked by a boy of around eleven to fifteen years of age. They would have been responsible for raking ashes from the grate and wheeling waste to the nearby dumps.

From the age of fifteen, the boys could then advance to tasks such as bringing coal to the calcining furnaces or the tipping of the calcined ore into the storage bunkers.

At seventeen, they were used to tough labour and the heat of the works and now assisted the furnacemen in collecting, weighing and loading.

By nineteen they were deemed ready to be in charge of their own furnace, though this would be as a calciner and they were apparently watched closely.

Working as calciners until about twenty-four, then they were considered for one of the final phases of the Welsh Process.

A man could then advance to the smelting of white metal, though this would only be entrusted to workmen of high abilities and superior workers may eventually advance to becoming a refiner.

These opportunities were scarce with only a handful of men likely to stand a chance of becoming a refiner.

There were rewards for experienced refiners. In 1820 William Harry renewed his agreement at the Llanelly works and was awarded £85 per year.

Some if they were trusted enough could possibly move into management.

A refiner at the Middle Bank Works became an assistant to the work's agent there, taking home a salary of £120.

Thomas Brown then made the move to the Upper Bank Works in 1820, stepping up to be a managing agent.

This hierarchy of jobs started to be reflected in the workers' pay. There was an expectation that the best workers also wanted a roof over their heads, and from the outset, company housing had been a feature of the Swansea district.

To house employees from the Forest Works, John Morris constructed Morris Castle in the form of a castellated apartment block in about 1770.

Williams and Grenfell did the same from 1793 to 1814, building forty terraced houses for their workers. White Rock subdivided a big house to accommodate ten families.

Not all workers were lucky enough to get company-owned homes, and employers began to make top up payments to them.

William Howell was a refiner at the Hafod Works, and there is record of him receiving ten guineas for every year that he did not receive a company cottage. Compensation for overtime work was also an option.

As was the custom of the time, adult men were the highest earners, but a number of households were sustained by earnings brought in by females or children of the house.

Evidence of women working in these times is hard to trace, but many people would have found employment within the copperworks, and women aged between twenty and forty were known to transport minerals in the works.

In works visited by Le Play, a group of seven women was bringing ore to the calcining furnaces by and in the course of a ten-hour shift, they transported around 150 tons of material between them.

Women could also be responsible for the removal of slag. To do this they would push trainloads of hot waste to the top of slag heaps. As a matter of fact, the works produced a lot more slag than actual copper. For example, the Middle Bank Works in 1828 existed on a seven-acre site, but its slag dump covered almost four times that requiring twenty-six acres.

In the early 1850s a visitor to the Hafod site found women's labour had started to phase out. If they had married or passed away, they were being replaced by boys and not other females. The slag tramming role had previously been carried out only by women.

That was just one of a number of supporting roles, for not everyone in the industry was a furnaceman. The works also employed artisans to help maintain the plant, including masons and carpenters.

But as we know it wasn't just the workers at the copperworks, there was a huge subsidiary operation involved. For example, all the colliers that worked on the coal side of things.

As mentioned before, in the early days of industry it was customary for copper companies to contract with colliery owners, Though arrangements were not always perfect as the owners would frequently demand that the copper companies only buy from them, as Thomas Popkin demanded of Robert Morris.

The copper masters in turn complained that their coal supply was inadequate. Considering the high importance of a reliable fuel supply, this led to some relationships being soured.

Smaller collieries could not keep up with the pace. Two of the leading firms, that of the Vivians and Williams Foster & Co, responded by collaborating with the Swansea Coal Co, a collection of mines in the lower Swansea Valley, employing around 450 colliers by 1841. Copper masters had to always be on the ball.

The copper boom also brought employment for seamen.

From the beginning the Swansea district relied upon ore that had been carried on vessels across the Bristol Channel, and these same vessels were used to carry coal to Cornwall. Though these would be too large to float upriver on the Tawe to the copperworks, the barks that arrived from Santiago de Cuba and Valparaiso had to discharge at quays on the lowest stretches of the Tawe closer to the town of Swansea.

Another support workforce was then tasked with dressing the ore and then taking it by barge to the different works that were further upstream.

This was hard repetitive work.

Work within the smelting halls did have a degree change, Thomas Cletcher, who inspected the Conham works towards the end of the 1690s, noted the Welsh Process had just three elements: roasting, smelting and refining.

However, by the nineteenth century a more complex multi-stage process had evolved with J.H. Vivian writing about the eight distinct steps required for the operation in the 1850s.

Most likely there would have been different revolutionary steps at different works, although there would have had to have been similarities.

John Vivian saw no uniformity, in his surveying of the Swansea district in the first decade of the nineteenth century, instead regarding the furnaces at the Middle Bank Works as unusually small and the Neath Abbey affairs as very singular.

Two decades later, the manager at the Hafod noted how different and distinct operations were at his works compared to those at Llanelly.

The copperworks would have been operating around the clock, other than when furnaces were cooling. Sunday or the Sabbath was the only day that work would be regularly ceased, though this was not always the case.

A week would start at six on a Monday morning and then continue on until four o'clock on Saturday afternoon, thus giving a work week of 130 hours.

By the 1840s many furnacemen worked twelve-hour days, swapping at six in the morning or six in the evening. Longer shift patterns had previously been noted, with men at the Neath Abbey Works being known to work twenty-four-hour shifts in 1796.

Le Play notes the twelve-hour shift pattern as the norm for many of the workers, besides calciners and furnacemen at level three, as they were required to work around the clock.

With the production of copper growing rapidly, the furnaces had to be scaled up and new divisions of labour were brought in to streamline things.

By the 1840s, a calciner was accompanied by three teenage barrow wheelers, each of which would deal with about ten tons of calcined ore in a ten-hour shift.

More workers led to more crowding. The copper masters tried to keep a tight control.

Furnacemen who failed to show for the start of their shift were fined a shilling a time if you worked at the Hafod Copperworks in the 1840s.

If you left work without any authorisation, you would also be fined, and unpaid shifts could happen if performance targets were not met.

I guess it was only natural then that workers were insisting on being issued with the right materials for the job, as they would be held to account should the results be deemed poor. The quality of coal was always a discussion.

Highly skilled workers were aware of their worth; they knew the current wages being paid across Swansea and were angry when shortchanged.

Skilled workers were averse to the type of regular attendance that the copper masters demanded. They annoyed their managers by abandoning the furnaces on traditional holidays such as Christmas.

Companies who contemplated wage reductions often waited until the harvest was in before they would act due to there being absentees around this time as earnings in the field were bumping up.

In the summer of 1830, the Swansea district companies came together in an agreement that wages were now higher there than any other trade, and for that reason they reckoned that a reduction should be made. However, the timing would be important, in order to avoid walkouts around harvest time.

The copper masters had some legal powers at their disposal when it came to dealing with workers.

There was labour legislation in Wales, such as the Statute of Artificers of 1563. It suggested that employment relations were of a private contract, the enforcement of said agreements were by judicial process, and there would be punishment for when a worker was uncooperative.

At the end of the 1790s, parliament passed the Combination Act which put a stop to any collective bargaining. It was refined in 1800. It enabled offending workers to be sent to jail via a conviction from a single magistrate. This was a crucial addition to powers already at the disposal for the copper masters in the Swansea district.

In 1820, a dispute broke out at the Middle Bank Works. The workers wanted higher wages and went on strike on 15 August. Williams and Grenfell returned an immediate counter action. The company had magistrates prosecute thirteen furnacemen under the Combination Act. These men were convicted for a conspiracy to raise their pay, which by today's standards sounds quite bizarre.

Two of the furnacemen were given three months in jail at Cardiff, with the remaining eleven being given two months hard labour at the Cowbridge House of Correction. Neither sounds appealing to me.

The strike spread alarm amongst the owners within the Swansea Valley. John Vivian of the Hafod Works wrote: 'I am very sorry to hear of riotous proceedings among the Middle Banks men ... for such conduct is contagious.'

He was proven right when not long after thirty-seven furnacemen left the Birmingham Cooper Company. Owners reached for their legal handbooks and John Vivian told his son to familiarize himself with the disciplinary recourses that were at his disposal, as he covered the day-to-day management at the Hafod Works.

With early industrial capitalism, workplace friction was a feature. Disputes were likely during times of rapid growth, when furnaces and workshops got extended.

Managers had to make certain that their return on capital investment went to the capital and not to labour. They feared that their workers would agree to an unspoken agreement to put a limit on output.

In the 1830s, the Hafod Works manager William Jones became convinced that his workers had come to the decision that they were making no more than six tons output daily. As there were some days when output was seven tons, in this instance, Jones thought that the sluggishness could be down to the extreme summer weather rather than a conscious desire.

The managers were always in fear that their workers would purposefully go slow.

A few weeks later at the Hafod Works, a worker named Enoch Thomas was bullying another worker. He was immediately fired.

William Jones was not just being paranoid, putting a limit on production was an understandable response to the ever-growing workloads.

The furnacemen were paid by the ton, but a lot depended on how a ton was defined. When the owners sold the copper, they did this in tons of twenty hundredweight. But the unit within the works was twenty-one hundredweight. The workers by this theory had to handle a ton that was five per cent heavier than the standard ton.

Of course, the employers tried to rationalize this by stating that the extra percentage represented the weight of the moisture in the ore, plus the weight of which it was carried within. Attempts to increase this further was less acceptable.

Attempts to do this however happened in the early 1840s when three convergent crises affected the works.

The first crisis was a global one: financial institutions looking for an outlet for over-accumulated capital was the catalyst. Funds were put in pursuit of any viable options. When the most plausible of these were exhausted, they turned towards ventures where the returns were uncertain. There were losses and credit destabilized more widely.

The crisis was aggravated by industrial restructuring and mechanisation.

In the turn of the 1840s, one sector after another began to topple into a twist of falling prices and contracting demand. The copper trade could not escape this downward pull.

In 1837, copper production in Britain was at 15,350 tons; in 1842 it had fallen to 9,940 tons.

The prices in the British copper markets followed the same trend.

The second crisis came in the form of politics.

Sir Robert Peel in 1842 introduced a budget to alleviate the unprecedented economic downturn. The budget's main principle was the reduction of duties; this did not apply to copper ore.

Lobbying by Cornish MPs had the duty of overseas ore raised, and the privilege of smelting in bond taken away, On the explanation that it afforded foreign manufacturers access to the British-made copper at cheaper prices that were not available to their British counterparts.

The Cuban and Chilean ores that had been a fixture on the Swansea scene since the late 1820s now were subjected to heavy import duties.

Smelters costs were rising and driven up even further by a third crisis.

It was a perennial concern for smelting copper companies to keep down the cost of furnace material. They were able to do this as they were few and close together, whereas the mine proprietors that they bought from were numerous and scattered.

Therefore, smelters could jointly act and impose their wants on the sellers of the ore.

However, in 1841, a new entrant, the English Copper Company did not abide to this arrangement, and as a result a bidding war ensued.

Now stuck between rising costs and shrinking revenues, Swansea copper owners tried to resolve this by cutting the one cost that they still had direct control over: labour.

This could be done by either lowering wages or increasing workloads, or a combination.

Increasing workloads was most achievable by the increasing of the weight of the material being used by the furnacemen; all furnacemen, besides calciners, were paid by the weight of the material output.

The workers at Hafod complained that the standard weight had been increased.

In July 1843, the copper masters announced that there would be wage cuts with considerable reductions across the board.

Strike action was to follow. It involved all the copperworks in the Swansea district, but also in the Neath and Afan Valleys.

Affected works along the Tawe included that of the Vivians at Hafod, the Grenfells at Middle Bank, the Forest Works of Benson, Logan and Co and White Rock.

The rural districts to the west of Swansea had already seen protest movements, like those of the Rebecca Riots, which were in response to the charges on tollgates, though they stood for more than just the tolls. There were also retributions to those who would not listen and change.

Magistrates were powerless in this insurgency. After burning down a tollhouse at Llanon in Carmarthenshire in 1843, the rioters then proceeded to smash the windows of a mansion constructed by Rees Goring Thomas, a magistrate, an impropriator of tithes, and a man connected to the copper industry. He was a shareholder in El Cobre mining association and two of his sons were partners at the Llanelly Copper Company.

This shows how the eastern riots of Rebecca could overlap with the west of the Swansea district.

The new poor law of 1834 added to Rebecca's grievances and in June 1834, hundreds of protestors descended upon Carmarthen. The townspeople joined in with them and together they laid ruin to the recently built workhouse there. Rumours began to circulate that Swansea was to receive something similar.

The introduction of the new pay scales at the copperworks was set for August, and a visit from Rebecca rioters was due to coincide with this decision. However, the rioters failed to show, perhaps mindful that the 75th regiment had hastily been assembled in the town.

This did not deter the copper workers from assembling in a show of strength. A large body of men marched on Swansea, numbering anywhere between 1,000 and 1,500. Before they managed to reach the town, they were met by police, the mayor and several employers.

Vivian persuaded the strikers to gather in a field above Hafod for an open-air meeting.

The Times reported that Vivian addressed the men and asked them to state their grievances. The workers spoke of pay, but Vivian described it as an act of necessity and that they could not afford to give more.

Workers complained that the hard nature of their work required them to have a good diet as working a furnace called for a remarkable calorie intake and the wage reductions would not allow this. They would rather be jobless and starve, than work hard and starve regardless.

It was pointed out that the Swansea district did not have a truck system where men were paid in tokens that had to be redeemed at a company store. The men were paid weekly in cash that allowed them to buy the protein rich diet that they needed.

Vivian is quoted as saying: 'I have always identified myself with the workmen ... I must express my surprise that my own men should join the others in the strike ...'

For the employers, the strike was an opportunity to help resolve a crisis where questions of local authority and international competitiveness were mixed.

For the workers, the strike was an attempt against the remorseless increase in their workloads, along with being a protest against the seniority system that prevailed within the industry.

Two workmen John Evans and David John spoke of their experiences in a letter published in *The Swansea Journal* in the first week of the strike. They denied that claims of extravagant pay for furnacemen were false, and that you would be on the lowest of wages for years before the chance to have a whole furnace. They noted that advancing was slow and for some of the men it never even came about.

Getting rid of the new pay scales would be no mean task. The furnacemen required unity among themselves. However, this would have been difficult as the employers had been extremely careful to make sure that the wage cuts varied widely.

They stated this was due to some work being more difficult so different roles would be hit differently. It is difficult not to see it as a tactical move aimed at dividing the workers.

A few of the workers at the Middle Bank Works appear to have worked throughout the strike and this was fatal to its cause. It led to a few men restarting work at Hafod during the last week of August, which prompted a night of violence.

On the following day, hundreds of the strikers congregated outside the Middle Bank Works in an attempt to picket out those at work. The riot act was invoked by magistrates in order to force their withdrawal.

Things became more desperate for those on strike by the start of September. The men had to help support their families and such.

By 7 September, the Hafod workers had agreed to go back to work at the original reduced rate proposed. By 11 September work had resumed right across the Swansea district.

Now that the copper masters had their way, they turned their attention to the regulation of the price of ore.

The Cornish market had been lacking stability since the English Copper Company had started the bidding war in the early 1840s.

The copper masters were happy that the first district wide strike would also be the last this industry saw. For the workers, who had eaten into their savings and whose best clothing and furniture were in pawn shops, things were difficult to swallow.

Swansea's time as a dominant player in the world of copper was eventful but short. The progressive fragmentation of the mid-nineteenth century that could be seen by the 1860s, became more cemented over the next three decades.

In one of the remaining copper companies in the Swansea district, an internal report was conducted, and it came to the stark realisation that Swansea was badly situated. It even thought about relocating the works, which was in deep contrast to when it had been able to use its locational advantages to assert control over the copper industry.

It was even more of a sting for Swansea because during this time of its decline, the world demand for copper was increasing. New developments in the electrical industry, construction of engines and other components of automobiles and locomotives all helped to stimulate the growth of the output from mines, mills and smelters.

The decline in Swansea in this time of growth led some people to argue that the Swansea copper companies must have had a series of business failures not to have been able to capitalize on this situation.

Understanding why Swansea's copper reign came to an end by the early twentieth century needs consideration of various complex factors, some of which would have been out of the control of the copper owners.

Swansea's geographical advantage of being a coal-blessed port was being undone due to new kinds of ore that did not require the full reverberatory furnace experience.

But there was also a geographical pull away overseas to contend with as there was a draw to the growing chemicals market from the metal refining business.

Swansea companies increasingly looked into the production of other metals or alloys, along with manufactured goods in order for them to sustain a business, but this brought added stress of direct competition with specialists who already had better links to those fast-evolving markets.

The electrical industry placed new demands upon the copper producers to surpass the conductivity of their product and to combat the new technologies, in particular those concerning wire drawing. This was difficult for Swansea companies who were rooted in traditional products and processes.

There was now a need for new equipment and new skills within the labour force, neither of which would be easy to implement at Swansea.

By the start of the twentieth century, the Swansea district was now working in an industry that had transformed in both scale and structure. Even though Swansea had undergone some business reorganisation, they were now matched either in size or capital by the bigger international companies that now operated in the sector.

The first big crisis to be acknowledged came in the late 1860s.

After the American Civil War, there was a period where copper prices fell. Smelting near the sites of the ore fields was on the increase around the world; the owners of the copper mines also had more choice when selling their product.

By 1860 it was becoming no longer the custom to send parcels of ore to Swansea for sale by public ticketing. Instead, private negotiations took place, thus greatly reducing Swansea's ability to control prices by working together.

Swansea had to put its collective voice aside and step away from their agreed amounts in a bid to secure their individual supplies of ore in an increasing market. Swansea lost ores and control over the prices.

To try to help the situation, some of the smelting companies attempted to reduce their costs and in October 1870, Williams, Foster & Co petitioned their landlord, the Duke of Beaufort, for a reduction in their rent on the Rose and Landore Works. But the value of land was rising within the lower Swansea Valley and demand for land for new industrial sites, such as the new Landore Steel in the early 1870s, increased prices. The duke didn't reduce the rent as he feared if he did this for one, he would end up doing this for many.

The Swansea copper owners tried to turn their attention to other ferrous metal, zinc in particular. Vivian and Sons opened their zinc smelter in 1868, and that same year, Pascoe and Sons started their own zinc smelting operations at Upper Bank. New zinc companies like Villiers Spelter & Co were also attracted to the district and set up in 1873.

Even so Swansea had to rely on outside technologies, like furnaces that had been developed in Belgium and Silesia, and experts were brought in to help in the early stages of the operations.

But shortcomings soon became visible, for example when complex ores like large zinc and lead deposits were discovered in South Australia.

Regarding copper smelting, the Swansea companies tried to focus on high grade ores, these required multiple-stage smelting to remove impurities. This could be more profitable, due to them still using the traditional furnace methods because these ores required a more fuel-intensive process.

By 1880 Newfoundland accounted for the biggest share of copper imports into Britain with over 22,000 tons, while South Africa was the second largest supplier at around the 15,800-ton mark. Swansea companies sought to extract additional value, particularly precious metals, from imported ores, as the copper content of the shipments declined.

H.H. Vivian drew upon experts recruited from Germany to develop methods for extracting silver from copper ores and mattes.

In 1870 Vivian & Sons and Williams, Foster & Co took over the White Rock site for silver and lead smelting.

The Swansea district was to remain a commercially viable presence in the global copper trade in the early 1880s, but in the late 1880s, there was a new expansion in the American copper ore mining industry. The opening up of new ore fields in Montana and Arizona gave sufficient supplies of copper to not only satisfy domestic demands, but also enough for use in export.

The United States were propelled into a good position of global dominance in copper production, withstanding other growing nations, and hence began a new era in the copper trade.

Some of the issues that Swansea copper companies faced were temporarily halted by the war years of 1914-1918.

The use of copper was prohibited other than in the production of munitions: explosives, guns, tanks, mortars and artillery.

Even though there were profits to be made during wartime, what would happen when the war was concluded soon loomed as a dark thought across the industry and government circles.

With legislation stopping the trade of copper with any enemy nations, it undermined the dominance German marketing firms had over copper purchasing in the later years of the nineteenth century. There was a hope to stop the dominance from reoccurring again after the war.

The Non-Ferrous Metals Trade Committee of the Board of Trade recommended that the government provide financial assistance for the development of copper refining in Britain. As a result, the British Metal Corporation was formed in 1918, with the outlook to continue state controls.

Companies that wished to trade in non-ferrous metals had to obtain a licence from the Board of Trade. It was hoped that this would be an answer to some of the issues being experienced by the United Kingdom's comparatively small companies.

After the war, a final push for the remaining copper companies to consider reorganisation was the collapse of prices in the world market in 1920.

The prices fell due to the declining demand for copper from previously key consuming countries such as Japan. Unemployment began to rise in copper-reliant manufacturing sectors.

The old companies were already struggling to compete with their new rivals. Vivian and Sons and Williams, Foster & Co came close to completely going out of business in the early 1920s. To find a solution, the two companies agreed to merge.

The British Copper Manufacturers Ltd was formed on 17 November 1924, consisting of assets from Williams, Foster & Co at Morfa and Middle Bank, and Vivian & Sons at Hafod and Taibach, along with Grice & Sons, a Birmingham tube-making company that Williams, Foster & Co owned. The practicalities of this new venture were discussed, at an important meeting in 1924 and it was acknowledged that whilst in the short-term Williams,

Foster & Co would run Morfa and Middle Bank and the Vivians at their works of Hafod and Taibach, it was proposed to ultimately close down the Middle Bank and Taibach works, in order to consolidate.

As the old family companies disappeared, and the number that were active reduced to a core of operations around Landore, the Swansea copper district's 200-year history faded away.

In its new formation, the Hafod-Morfa works continued in metal fabrication operations.

Many of the original copper operations that were spread along the banks of the River Tawe became derelict after being abandoned by the 1960s. The remaining Hafod-Morfa company stopped operations in 1980.

With the smelting operations and processing plants closing their doors, the cumulative effect of 200 years of intense pollution of the soil, vegetation and landscape lay exposed for public scrutiny.

There was a coming together of groups that wished to tackle the problem of this derelict wasteland. A project team was established in 1961, made up of council members, academics and representatives from local groups to survey the area and put a report together for redevelopment.

This started in the early 1960s with an in-depth tree-planting programme that even included some local school children and community groups.

The report of the area envisioned new housing, new industries, areas for recreation and commercial developments that were all be connected via the construction of a new valley access road. There was the hope that new life could be breathed into the area.

Though this vision did not have a place for the remembrance of the industrial legacy of Swansea copper, the chimney stacks and furnace halls stood as symbols of the reason the land was blighted and toxic. Their removal was part of the process of renewal of the time.

With the former copperworks branded as hideous, the site clearance was a priority, and a local division of the Territorial Army was brought in to use the ruined buildings for demolition and explosives training.

There was little enthusiasm in the 1960s in Britain for keeping industrial buildings for heritage value.

There were however arches of the White Rock works that were strangely elegant, and people felt should have been preserved, but they also met their fate via the demolition team.

By the start of the millennium, only a small portion of buildings remained on the sides of the Tawe, such as a chimney stack and engine shed of the Vivian and Sons Hafod works, and Morfa buildings that housed a laboratory and canteen.

The surrounding area is newly green and home to a football stadium, retail outlets, restaurants and a park and ride.

More recently the historic Hafod-Morfa Works has seen Penderyn open a new operational distillery and shop there.

But there is also more in the works for the area, a laboratory building and the engine houses of the Musgrove and the Vivian engines are next in line to be restored.

A restaurant is planned for the old laboratory space, while the engine houses will become a heritage attraction along with a café.

The Penderyn Distillery that has opened on the site of Swansea Copperworks, followed an in-depth restoration and preservation project on site, due to a collaborative effort from Penderyn Distillery, Swansea council, Swansea University, the John Weaver Contractors and funding sources.

To access this area, you are in luck as it is located right by Swansea city's park and ride, and from here you can explore both sides of the River Tawe.

Before concluding this chapter, I would like to share an interesting anecdote uncovered during my research. On a walk with the Friends of Hafod Morfa Copper, they mentioned that the Hafod works and the Morfa works were so close that workers from each site were cautioned against conversing with those from the other, lest they reveal trade secrets.

During research, I also met Margaret, a remarkable lady aged 101. She recounted how her father worked at Swansea Copperworks. Although Margaret was unsure of the exact location where her father worked – his retirement certificate states ICI, a company that eventually absorbed some of the copper works – she mentioned that he worked in the lower Swansea valley near the River Tawe, in the engine house. She fondly recalled her father's love for the engine under his care, while humorously noting her mother's displeasure when her father used one of her best blouses to polish the engine. With Margaret's permission, I have included her story and a photograph of her father's retirement certificate on the next page.

Margaret's father's retirement certificate indicates that he worked for ICI, which took over some of the copper works. However, due to Margaret's

A retirement certificate awarded to Sydney Morgan Bevan when he retired from working within the ICI, the company that had taken over some of the copper works in Swansea.

uncertainty about whether he worked for the copper works before ICI or solely for ICI, the details remain ambiguous. What remains vivid in her memory is the blouse incident.

Research on the Swansea Museum website indicates that British Copper Manufacturers owned the combined works of Hafod and Morfa until 1928, despite copper refining ceasing around 1924. The site later came under Yorkshire Imperial Metals, a fusion of ICI and Yorkshire Metals, in 1957. These merged works continued operating until their closure in August 1980.

A section of the River Tawe in Swansea.

CHAPTER SIX

The Rebecca Riots

The roads of Great Britain were in a terrible condition in the seventeenth century. In 1764 parliament passed an act to remedy the deplorable roads. The act brought together a formation of trusts in which the wealthy were required to invest money, to repair, improve and maintain the roads in their areas; and enabled the erection of barriers that would enable them to charge tolls upon people who used the roads.

The roads did indeed start improving, but the tolls literally began to take their toll, especially on farmers. Each of the trusts was able to set their own toll rates and they displayed the charges on a board attached to their tollhouse.

There was however a maximum that could be charged, fixed by the government and could only be raised by acts of parliament.

In 1839, a toll for a horse-drawn carriage was six pence, and one shilling six pence for a score of cattle. Considering that a farm labourer earned about ten shillings per week, these charges were quite high.

People could be paying the same toll repeatedly during a day, making it extremely costly.

Typically, people felt resentful towards tollgates, although complaining would not alter the situation.

There was already unrest in the 1830s and 1840s within South Wales due to a few bad harvests, a shortage of food, trade depressions and riots and strikes in industrial areas.

Chartists were everywhere and wanted the lower classes to have their voices heard in parliament.

The farm communities in West Wales had many grievances, such as paying high rents, church rates, tithes, tolls and the effects of the poor law.

The tollgates became physical objects on which farmers could take out their frustrations.

In the summer of 1839, this exploded into acts of violence and destruction when some farmers in West Wales started to destroy the much-hated tollgates along with tollhouses. They blackened their faces and sometimes wore women's clothing. These men became known as the Rebeccaites, or Rebecca's Daughters and the leaders of this unrest, Rebecca or Becca.

These first attacks were short-lived and the Rebeccaites fell silent until October 1842.

Rebecca had even turned her attention to more symbols of oppression, like the workhouse at Carmarthen in the summer of 1843.

We have newspaper articles that provide us with information surrounding the riots.

On 8 July 1842, *The Cambrian* newspaper reported that a tollgate had been destroyed and that the unrest of Carmarthenshire, Cardiganshire and Pembrokeshire had now reached Glamorganshire. This was only a brief report, and later evidence informs us that on this occasion, the leader here was Daniel Lewis, a local weaver and most likely employed by one of the seven mills in the Pontarddulais region.

Under his leadership a group of the Rebeccaites attacked the Bolgoed Gate near to the Fountain Inn on the main road of Pontarddulais. It is said that the attack had been organized in meetings held at the inn.

The fiancée of Daniel Lewis, Elizabeth watched the attack from a window on the upper floor of the inn.

In August, *The Cambrian* reported that an investigation was held before magistrates at the town hall in Swansea, on Wednesday, 2 August.

Evidence was given by an informant named John Jones. He had been present during the attack on the Bolgoed Gate. When asked if he could speak

English, he replied no, in English, which resulted in laughter. Mr Glasbrook was brought in as an interpreter.

Jones spoke of how he was a farm labourer and lived at Cwmsciach, and then at a later point, that he had lived for the last six weeks in a barn that belonged to Morgan Pugh. He claimed that he saw the destruction of the gate in the early hours of the morning between twelve and one. He described the men involved as some wearing white shirts, but others wearing women's bed gowns and women's caps. He noted that guns had been present.

Jones described how the tollbar was cut with cross-saws and handsaws and the tollhouse was destroyed thanks to the removal of lower stones by pickaxes. He also stated how one person rode upon a white horse, was addressed by the others as 'mother' and gave directions and a small speech.

Jones pointed out Daniel Lewis to be that man. He recognized more people involved, like Griffith Vaughan of Pontarddulais, John Morgan and David Jones.

He stated how he met the crowd of rioters at the lowest part of Goppa Mountain and then accompanied them to the Bolgoed Gate.

Jones was then cross examined by a number of solicitors on behalf of the four men that Jones had given information on. His responses were sometimes inconsistent with what he had previously said.

According to a government solicitor named Maule, all four men that Jones mentioned were to be charged with a misdemeanour for their alleged involvement. However, several witnesses proved that Jones' testimony was not credible.

At the end of the investigation, the defendants were arraigned for trial at the next assize and having agreed to appear at such a time, they were liberated.

The Rebecca Riots were becoming more and more violent. *The Cambrian* reported on an attack on the Pontarddulais Bridge Gate. The attack took place during the night of Wednesday, 6 September and the early morning hours of the following day.

Nearly all the people involved appeared to have come from Carmarthenshire, where it's suggested that men were obliged to take part due to threats.

The Cambrian noted that people were called to assemble near Llanon on the Wednesday.

Eyewitness accounts claimed the Rebeccaites marched along blowing their horns and firing their guns. They claimed there was a minimum of 100 horses involved, many of them carrying two people. They were led by a Rebecca figurehead and her daughters under the guise of white dresses and bonnets.

As they neared Pontarddulais, their arrival was announced to the gatekeeper by yelling and the firing of their guns. The gatekeeper quickly moved furniture into the garden. When he could see the mob in his eye-line, he ran away hiding himself in a field around 100 yards from the gate.

On arrival at the gate, the rioters smashed the windows and door of the house, completely ransacking the interior.

Though the authorities were aware of the intentions of the rioters, their response was in two parts. They sent magistrates, police and troops from Swansea to Pontarddulais, and magistrates along with troops from Llanelly to the Hendy Bridge Gate.

Invoking magistrates was to enable civil guidance on which troops could act.

The Cambrian provides us with an account of these events. It reports that a rural police force, including Superintendent Peake, two sergeants and four police officers headed towards the Pontarddulais Gate. They were quickly accompanied by Captain Napier.

In the distance was the sound of guns, rockets, horns and a huge number of horses, as well as a voice that reportedly made a horrible, indescribable noise. It was noted that three cheers were given when the rioters were near the gate.

The attack began with items such as saws and sledges. They were quickly successful in breaking down the gate and then turned attentions toward the tollhouse. They demolished it by breaking the windows and knocking down the door. However, the gateposts remained.

At this point of the riot, the magistrates and the armed police made their advancement. The Rebeccaites assembled with most of them on horseback, an estimated number of about 150 to 200.

All the people involved in the riot were disguised with blackened faces or women's clothing or white shirts or bonnets; some seemed to have their coats turned inside-out. It was reported that in this attack the Rebecca leader wore a large, white cloak.

When the police appeared, the rioters met them with a round of fire, though this was without any effect. The police responded with fire also and a conflict quickly escalated the closer these two groups got.

After about fifteen minutes the mob began to retreat and disperse in all different directions. Three members of the mob were captured, including the leader of the riot, John Hughes, who was badly wounded.

Four rioters were also captured whilst they tried to make their escape; they'd been met by an infantry unit that had come from Llanelly.

The wounded were attended to by Dr Bird, who ordered them to be taken via stretchers to the hospital at the Swansea House of Correction.

At another time, *The Cambrian* reported on the investigation that took place in which Captain Napier gave his evidence which gives a good indication of what happened at Pontarddulais, though of course as Captain Napier saw them.

Napier had recovered from the injuries he had received at Cwmcillau farm. He stated that he accompanied Superintendent Peake, along with two sergeants and four police officers to Pontarddulais, and he heard the guns and horns going off. Also, that he heard someone shout 'Come come' from the direction of the Red Lion Inn that was just a short distance from the turnpike gate.

Napier then heard someone shout loudly, 'Gate!' followed by noises of destruction. With this Napier stated, he along with officers headed toward the gate, and after appearing in view, Napier noted he saw men on horseback, most of them in women's clothing, with blackened faces.

A group of the men dismounted and began breaking both the gate and the tollhouse. He also commented on the continued fire of guns. He instructed his men to proceed toward the rioters on horses. He reports that one of the men on horseback turned towards him and fired their pistol at him. Napier moved on and fire was aimed in the direction of the police.

During the cross-examination of Napier, he said John Hughes was the person who fired his gun at him and that he believed Hughes was one of three men who turned and rode at the police.

When discussing David Jones, Napier said he saw Jones violently resisting against Lewis Llewellyn Dillwyn, the magistrate, and police. It was noted that Jones was hit on the head several times before he was taken away.

The police who were present also gave their testimonies. Some evidence provided by them appears to be contradictory by way of more than one officer claiming to have arrested the same prisoner.

For example, PC Wright and Captain Napier gave slightly different accounts for prisoner John Hughes.

Wright stated Hughes had a gun in his hand and fired towards the authorities; Hughes then dismounted and ran off with his horse; whereas Napier said he had shot Hughes' horse and that he had picked up Hughes' dropped pistol, though PC Price said something else.

Price stated he removed John Hughes from his horse and gave him over to Sergeant Jenkins. Then Price claimed to have taken the prisoner Hughes who was suffering from a broken arm, though this was not true. Price alleged to have taken Hughes into custody near the Pontarddulais Inn.

David Jones was not one of the men upon horseback that rode towards police, but he was arrested, having been shot seven times in the back. *The Cambrian* stated this was proof that the rioters had actually fired at each other, perhaps due to confusion or possibly intentionally. The bullets that caused his wounds were not used by the police.

PC Williams claimed David Jones and another rioter came out of the tollhouse and that he was struck by an iron bar; he retaliated by cutting the man on his head and then running away, but Sergeant George Jones apprehended him.

Sergeant Jones claimed he first noticed David Jones running out of the tollhouse, he then pursued him and grabbed him. This resulted in a bit of a scuffle and Jones got away. But the sergeant once again got hold of Jones and this time was able to keep him in custody and handcuff him.

On 9 September, nine magistrates undertook a private investigation at the house of correction in Swansea, regarding these claims and charges. The involvement of John Hughes, John Hugh and David Jones in the destruction of the Pontarddulais Gate was looked into.

On the following Monday, the three prisoners were present in the town hall for public examination. David Jones had his head bound in bandages; John Hughes was present with his arm in a sling; and John Hugh wore his gown and straw hat to the proceedings.

John Hughes was the son of a farmer, whose farm Ty Isha was near Tumble in Carmarthenshire. He was around twenty-four and was described as both powerful and good looking. The consensus is that he was the Rebecca at Pontarddulais that night.

John Hugh, another son of a farmer, resided near Llanon. He was a little older and was described as being married and able to read a little.

There is little known regarding David Jones. He was about twenty-one and was most likely illiterate.

The men that had been captured by the Llanelly contingent were people like Lewis Davis who alleged that he had been compelled to accompany the mob after threats from about ten or so people, who called for him with guns.

Another that had been apprehended was William Hugh, a fourteen-year-old farmer's son. He claimed to have been in bed when a crowd gathered outside his home compelling him to go along with them. He maintained that he proceeded to put on his own clothing, but they dressed him in women's clothing and gave him a horn. When the opportunity presented itself, he turned back and was met by the troops that apprehended him.

Another prisoner was Henry Rogers, a farm servant, who claimed that he was only present as he had just gone to see the mob. Thomas Williams, a servant to John Thomas at Llangennech Mill, also accompanied Rogers and was caught whilst returning home. These two men were not disguised and were not wearing any women's clothing when they were taken into custody.

The chief magistrate told both Rogers and Williams that they would be discharged due to there not be enough evidence regarding them.

John Hughes, John Hugh and David Jones were kept on remand until the following day when they underwent their final examination. The charges against them were read out, these being the riots and unlawfully demolishing the tollhouse, while John Hughes was also under the charge of having a loaded pistol and firing it at Napier with intent. David Jones and John Hugh were said to have aided and abetted him. The chairman announced to the prisoners that they would stand trial at the next assize.

Within the Lordship of Gower and Kilvey there were two turnpike trusts: the Swansea Turnpike Trust and the Wych Tree Bridge Trust.

The Swansea one was the larger of the two, being responsible for seventy-seven miles of turnpike roads that included three miles in Swansea.

On 7 September, the Swansea Trust made up of magistrates, landlords and landowners conducted a meeting with an aim to provide some relief to the payers of the toll. The main idea involved taking over the running of the Wych Tree Bridge Trust which was responsible for two-and-half miles and the bridge. The resolution here was to discontinue this gate, as well as others, including the Bolgoed Gate.

A debate ensued and one trustee opposed this proposal as he felt it would lead the farmers to believe that the trustees had acted out of fear. Another trustee stated he would have felt similarly if it were not for the proceedings at Pontarddulais and thought it had come time for concessions to be made.

The Pontarddulais shootout appears to have established caution amongst the Rebeccaites of the local area, although this would not be enough to deter them from their cause and they began adapting new approaches.

The Cambrian reported on 23 September that a temporary gate had been erected at Pontarddulais after being destroyed the night of the shootout. The trustees had put a bar in place as a temporary substitute for the missing gate.

Information was received by the authorities that an attack on the bar was intended to take place on a Saturday night.

Consequently, it was watched closely and Rebecca was a no show on the night in question. However, just the following night, once the military had abandoned their posts, Rebecca and her daughters removed the temporary bar.

By the Wednesday, new gates had been installed although the paper wondered how long they would last. The new toll collector received a letter suggesting he quit or face the consequences.

In order to help combat the riots, the military was ramped up again and in a letter to the Prime Minister, towards the end of September, the Home Secretary disapproved of the commanding chief of all the military forces in South Wales Colonel Love for his handling over the situation.

The letter said that though Colonel Love had 1,800 men under his command, the Home Secretary was not happy with how he was making use of this force. The letter continued to make his opinions clear, implying that the force should be sufficient to cover the four counties, which the colonel had seemingly been asked to keep peaceful, though it appears that the force was kept in constant motion and always late to arrive to the disturbances. The Home Secretary argued furthermore that if an instance occurred, the colonel would only send soldiers to that area the following day.

By October, there was a noted reduction in attacks that were being carried out by Rebecca and her many daughters due to a number of factors.

At the end of July, it was known that the government was prepared to hear people's concerns and grievances.

In August, increasing numbers gave their support to meetings and other non-violent activities in order to get their point across.

On 2 October, Queen Victoria signed a proclamation, consisting of a reward system whereby £500 was to be given to anyone who was willing to uncover and apprehend any perpetrators of any Rebecca doings.

The aim of this was to encourage the law enforcing officers to increase their efforts in dealing with the perpetrators. Captain Napier fitted into this category. He had not been receiving good press, with one London newspaper ridiculing him as the villain for gunning down farmers and their sons along with their horses. Parliament did give Napier £500 and passed a vote of thanks for his services to the cause.

A smaller award accompanied by a pardon was aimed at encouraging lawbreaking people, excepting actual perpetrators, to turn each other in. This resulted in some arrests when unscrupulous men informed on others before someone had the chance to inform on them.

On 25 October, a Royal Commission of three men arrived in Carmarthen to set off on a tour of South Wales. The aim of the commission was to get to the root cause of the discontent and even more importantly to put forward a recommendation to resolve the situation.

To complete this work, the Royal Commission took around five months. At the same time, another Royal Commission concentrated on the more controversial and politically sensitive aspects of the inquiry.

If the assize court was held in Swansea, the jury would be made up of local people, but with the risk of them being intimidated or even actually being sympathetic to the prisoners awaiting trial, it was decided to hold the trials in Cardiff. Due to the seriousness of the situation it was also decided that the trials should not wait for the customary spring assize and instead be held by special commission. On 26 October the special commission opened at Cardiff's town hall.

For security, there was a detachment from the top division of London police present when the government-appointed judges arrived. Seventy-five-year-old Bain Gurney and Sir Cresswell, described as younger and more charitable, arrived at eleven in the high sheriff's carriage, along with several of the neighbouring gentry in their carriages.

They proceeded to the town hall to begin the commission, and the court was then adjourned until two o'clock.

Seventeen people were to stand before the judges, though it's said that the people who were facing a lesser charge of destroying certain gates would not have to be tried.

All the men were there ready to surrender themselves if or when necessary. Representing the defendants was M.D. Hill, QC a law reformer, along with three barristers.

The judges took their places on the bench just after two. The jury list was then called out, although there were difficulties raised as a number of people actually refused to stand. Eventually the jury consisted of gentlemen and tradesmen from both Cardiff and Merthyr; farmers were excluded from this.

John Hughes was addressed on 2 November. His charges were read out: he had acted unlawfully; he disturbed the peace; by use of force, he had started to pull down the tollhouse of William Lewis; and that he shot at Captain Napier with intent. Hughes pleaded not guilty.

Unfortunately for him there was not a great deal of real defence evidence. Some of the verbal evidence that was presented gives us an indication of what happened that night in Pontarddulais.

It is said that Captain Napier stated that he had been told information around four in the evening, and due to this received intelligence he and his men made their way across the country, beginning at Penllergaer, then proceeding to walk around ten miles by foot. By this point the captain claimed he heard the noises from the Rebeccaites, all the horns and firing of pistols. Napier stopped in a field around 600 yards from the gate intended for an attack, when he heard voices from the Carmarthenshire side of the river. The noise grew dramatically louder and came from the direction of the Red Lion Inn.

At ten to one in the morning, Napier heard sounds of the gate being broken and the smashing of glass. Napier alleged he then ordered his men to follow him and proceeded across the lane and then into the main road.

On the following day, the counsel for the defence spoke to the jury referring to the evidence that Captain Napier had given. The defence claimed that after receiving the intelligence of an intended attack as early as four pm, instead of trying to prevent the riot from happening, they chose rather to hide away in a field until the gate was actually broken.

The defence alleged that the magistrates and police had wasted an opportunity to prevent an outrage of the law, and instead actively chose to wait to see it was committed. The main claim here was that Captain Napier had just wanted to make arrests rather than prevent crime itself.

Napier described that he saw three men on horseback, disguised and facing the tollhouse and claimed the men appeared to be directing others on the opposite side of the gate. Napier then told his men to fall in and head towards the party, with Napier yelling out 'Stop!'

A man on hearing this fired at Napier and the captain ordered that man to be watched; he shot the man's horse. The man then fell from his horse and Napier claimed they both had a scuffle. The man was then wounded in his arm by someone unknown to Napier who said he did not take said person into custody and was hit on the back of the head by a stick and that this attacker was later taken into custody by one of the police officers.

The next day, eleven witnesses were called in and provided the prisoner a character reference of general good conduct and obedience in regard to laws. But this was to no avail as the jury returned after around just twenty minutes of deliberations with a verdict of guilty, along with a recommendation of mercy due the accounts of previous good character.

The sentencing was deferred till the Monday, and it would become all too clear that mercy was not a word that Judge Gurney understood.

The trial then continued with the Morgan family with the charge that they had assaulted Captain Napier when he was carrying out his duties and for having attempted to prevent the lawful apprehension of one Henry Morgan.

The attorney general admitted that he would not bring to sentence the parents Morgan and Esther Morgan, but he felt that for the rest some sentence would be commensurate with the offence.

Margaret Morgan was sentenced to six months in prison; Rees and John Morgan were sentenced to twelve months imprisonment.

Another prisoner Lewis Davies pleaded guilty to having along with others assisted in the demolition of the Pontarddulais Gate, though the attorney general allowed the defendant to be discharged as long as he was willing to appear at a later date.

A no show of a witness may have been why the trial of six other men from the Gower did not go ahead, with it being deferred until the spring.

These six men were suspected of being involved in the damaging of the Bolgoed Gate as well as the Rhyd-y-Pandy Gate.

The only witness to the men's involvement was John Jones the informer and if he was a no show at the trial, then the prosecution would not have been able to proceed to a conviction.

The Cambrian reported just before Christmas that John Hugh, John Hughes and David Jones who were convicted in Cardiff for the destruction of the Pontarddulais Bridge Tollhouse were sent on 7 December to be taken to prison. This would be the last time the paper made any reference to these three prisoners.

These men were briefly taken to Millbank Penitentiary in London where they underwent three months of extensive discipline and solitude where even the guards were not allowed to speak to them.

Queen Victoria began to receive petitions begging for a reduction in the sentencing of John Hughes, some sent by his mother and even members of the jury who had found him to be guilty, but these would not amount to anything.

The three men were placed on board a convict ship and set sail on a horrible four-month voyage to Van Diemen's Land, modern-day Tasmania. The men reached their destination on 10 July, but just a week later David Jones was dead.

John Hugh ended up serving his seven-year stint as a slave and was set free in December 1850. He later married a convict woman, perhaps by this point his Carmarthenshire wife had passed away.

John Hughes ended up serving thirteen-and-a-half years of his set twenty-year sentence and was given a conditional pardon in 1857. He wrote home frequently but never made the return journey. He married and made a nice life for himself, passing away aged eighty-two.

Back in South Wales, the remaining seven suspects appeared at the Glamorgan Spring Assize.

In March 1844, the charges against Griffith Vaughan, William Morgan, David Jones and Daniel Lewis regarding their suspected involvement in attack on the Bolgoed Gate were dropped and no further charges were brought against other alleged participation in the destruction of the Rhyd-y-Pandy Gate.

The reasons behind this are not known, it was most likely due to the informer John Jones being either discredited as a witness or that he failed to show up at court completely and then prosecution would have been left without its only witness.

Under the terms of the Queen's proclamation in July 1844, the Swansea magistrates had to give John Jones a gratuity of £20.

By April 1846, *The Cambrian* reported that the former informer John Jones was arrested by police on a charge of stealing a pan made of brass at Pontarddulais. He was tried at Carmarthen and was acquitted. He had admitted guilt to Sergeant Bennet of the Swansea police, who had apprehended Jones after spotting him trying to sell the article in question. Bennet was not brought in as a witness and thereafter John Jones disappears from the records.

On 6 March 1844, the report of the commission of inquiry was published. It stated that the commissioners gathered at Carmarthen on 25 October and terminated the inquiries at Merthyr-Tydfil on 13 December.

The report declared that the riots were not connected with political causes but were first driven by a sense of local grievance and that this was exploited in some instances by people with evil motives. The main issues of complaint were founded on the mismanagement of funds made from turnpike roads and the frequency with which these were collected.

But the report alluded that things like tithes, rent, and the poor law added to the problem along with the reduction in capital for farmers due to bad harvests and the price of cattle and butter decreasing.

It concluded that to help remove the discontent, important changes needed to be made with regards to laws related to roads. They claimed to agree that those who used the roads should in turn help with their upkeep.

The proposal was that Carmarthen, Pembroke and Glamorgan establish consolidated trusts for each county and a uniform rate be set at a moderate amount. The frequency of the demands for payments should be done away with, although should the money collected from the gates be insufficient to cover all the expenses, then it would be made up by a rate on all property. It also wished to repeal the laws in South Wales around the regulation of turnpike roads and the placement of each trust in each county to be under a general executive, which later became known as the Roads Board.

A rule they felt important was that a toll should not be laid more than once in seven or eight miles within the same county.

Due to certain difficulties the new Glamorgan Road Board only came into existence in 1845, by this time lots of the tollgates in the Lordship of Gower and Kilvey had ceased operating.

Some other gates did remain in place for around thirty years, mainly to pay the debts of the old turnpike trusts.

By 1876, the last remaining gates were discontinued, and those roads were taken over by the Glamorgan Highways Board.

Arguably Rebecca had achieved her goal with the removal of any unnecessary gates, a reduction in the rate of the tolls and a revolution of the arbitrary powers of the turnpike trustees. But above everything else, the government had been forced to listen and ordered to remedy the situation.

Although some had received harsh sentences and ratepayers were stuck with expenses for years to come, such as those connected with the billeting of the troops, on the whole, Rebecca was largely a people's protest and one that is firmly cemented within Welsh history.

A stone in Pontraddulias to mark the Bologoed Gate.

CHAPTER SEVEN

Swansea Docks

There are many carparks in and around Swansea Marina and the SA1 postcode area that will allow you to park and explore on foot the history mentioned in this chapter.

Growing up in Swansea, I have often walked through the marina and dockland areas without even thinking of how bustling and busy it used to be and how many people from all walks of life and places graced this area. But there was me, just using it as a route to get from A to B. I suppose sometimes the things or places you see every day lead you to take them for granted, though as I get older, I begin to understand the grand scale and importance of the history that has happened here.

Not only have I grown up around this area, I am also a granddaughter and daughter of dock workers.

Swansea has been used as a port as far back as medieval times. It dealt with exports such as coal and culm and imports like foods, cloth, wine and of course, copper ore.

Swansea's growth into the Copperopolis resulted in quays being placed along the sides of the River Tawe for around three miles up-river.

There was a great need for a proper dock where cargo could easily be unloaded and loaded, no matter what the state of the tide. People wanted

This is a photograph that I took of the Sails Bridge in Swansea Marina.

A photograph I took whilst walking around the area of the Prince of Wales Dock area.

to ship their cargo without being ruled by the forces of nature. The phrase 'time is money' springs to mind.

There was rapidly growing pressure from shipowners and industrialists to create a float or wet dock. The good visibility at Swansea city's eastern gateway lends itself to the view that it was the east side where the Swansea docks started life.

Hindsight is a wonderful thing and probably suggests this is what should have happened, however with the minor exceptions of a small shipping area with quay walls at Port Tennant, which itself was subsequently compromised by the tide, they did not start there.

The Tawe River that runs through Swansea was actually able to be navigated for nearly 5km upstream, though only at high tide. This is where the first quaysides were constructed, evidence of which is still visible today, although this was not without its disadvantages: for example the expenses, inconvenience and the risks that were involved in having your vessel laying upon river mud when the tide was out. This was one of the reasons behind the demands from the traders and industrialists for a floating harbour.

However, before the 1790s, other things had got in the way, like the conservative burgesses being too occupied with accruing personal wealth and continually refusing to give their approval of such demands.

Gabriel Powell, a steward to the Duke of Beaufort, was strongly opposed to the area of turning industrial rather than keeping the seaside. When he passed away in 1788, a major obstacle to improvements at the harbour was out of the way, though progress was incredibly slow.

The discussions around a proposed dock alongside the strand took much time to reach realisation.

The Tawe was aligned with the New Cut creation, that opened up in 1845. As a result, the bow of the River Tawe left became known as the North Dock and this opened in 1852. This was to be Swansea's first permanent water-filled dock.

It exported coal from the western side and patent fuel from its eastern side, where there were also copper ore yards and grain warehouses. In its heyday, this dock was able to be walked across from ship to ship.

While work was moving forward on the creation of the North Dock, discussions were also taking place about the construction of another wet dock on the Burrows. The work on this started in 1852. Even though there were problems, such as a change in ownership, the South Dock opened in 1859.

The North Dock became redundant and closed in 1928 with just its basin being kept for the ships mooring at Weavers flour mill.

The North Docks half-tide basin was towards the south of the area known today known as Quay Parade. After the Weavers mill closed in 1963, the basin was filled in and by the 1970s it would frequently become the home to caravans and groups from the traveller community. Today a Sainsbury's supermarket occupies the site.

At Sainsbury's café extension, you are able to see the point where this basin connected with the River Tawe. Two sets of four cast-iron mooring bollards remain, with curved characteristics on the ground that mark each side of the entrance to the basin.

A number of the bollards that can be found around the maritime quarter and on the riverbanks are embossed SHT, which stands for Swansea Harbour Trust, the body in charge of the port from 1792 until 1923. The Great Western Railway Company then took over the management.

The bollards are dated as to when they were put in place and this helps paint the historical picture of the area.

The building of the North Dock caused acute frustration to copper master John Henry Vivian and led him to form a company to construct a masonry dock on the seafront of Swansea, in an area that was once known as Burrows.

The eastern area of the Burrows had been a location of early nineteenth century politeness and gentility and as a result many people there were terribly upset by the idea that their splendid pleasure gardens could potentially become a vast hole with steam engines noisily thundering and thumping around the place where elegant Georgian terraces once stood. Quite the contrast in their eyes.

However, they were not able to argue against progress and William Clark Russell is quoted in 1882 as saying, 'one must not think of beautiful ... but of the useful.' He goes on to mention how people spoke about how many ships there were and how much imports and exports there were rather than the views of the sea or mountain ranges. Perhaps his viewpoint in today's world would have been different due to the current climate.

To put it into perspective, just under 80,000 people came out in 1853 to witness the first bit of turf lifted by the Marquess of Worcester. However, it was not to be until 1859, after a run of disputes, strikes, financial issues and the takeover of the harbour trust that they opened the South Dock.

Coal was exported from the north side of the dock and towards the western end stood timber yards. Fish were imported to the south side of the basin as there was a fish market there, which remains in use today, freshly stocked, of course.

The opening of the South Dock was recorded in *The Cambrian* as more important than anything gone before, making Swansea an industrial and commercial place. However, it would become abundantly clear in the 1870s that two wet side docks were not enough to keep up with the fast and demanding nature of Swansea's flourishing coal, copper and other metal trades.

South Dock continued its service due to it being the base for Swansea's trawlers and was also the location of the fish market.

South Dock closed down in 1969 and became partly filled in.

Although about five years later, this dock's potential was realized with the Swansea council deciding to excavate the in-fill, allowing the sea to flow back into the basin and create a marina to house around 600 boats and yachts. This would become a central piece of the new maritime quarter in Swansea that included houses, food outlets and some other amenities.

On the east side of the River Tawe, there were three docks all linked: the Prince of Wales Dock; the Kings Dock; and the Queens Dock.

The construction started from 1879, completely obliterating the inlet and its natural habitat known as Fabian's Bay. Today, Swansea's noisiest, busiest and most polluting roads renamed after what once most likely would have been a pretty and idyllic area. The bay itself had taken its name from the family of Daniel Fabian who had moved from Llandrhidian in 1639, to the St Thomas area in order to farm at Glanybad. Their farmhouse became a very important and useful landmark for ships that made their way into what was a natural harbour.

The farmhouse would quickly become known as Fabian's House. It was sadly destroyed in 1850.

There is another Swansea landmark in this area at the furthest eastern end of the inlet, and this is the Salt House, where salt was evaporated out of the seawater. It was in this area that Swansea's first eastern pier was built.

A smaller west pier was then built on the other side of Fabian's Bay. These two piers converged in a pincer-type formation.

Other than the 70m gap between the pier heads, Fabian's Bay had become an enclosed area and a shelter for idle vessels. However, its use as an operational harbour was highly restricted and dependent on the tides.

The piers no longer stand at Fabian's Bay, just platforms of stone now just sitting idly in the river not far from the place where until 2006 the Swansea-Cork Superferry used to dock.

The pierhead is stranded by a Victorian slipway that cut through the old pier, providing a platform for the harbour's one o'clock gun.

Swansea Harbour Trust was concerned about the increasing incapacity of the west side docks and had they cooperated with George Tennant in developing his shipping place on the eastern end of Fabian's Bay, they could have possibly found a fitting area for the east side extension.

Though when the trustees were ready to act, a lot of the site had been sold to the Lambert family for them to use for a copper ore smelting factory.

That they had delayed action meant that there was barely any space left resulting in the new dock taking up a lot of Port Tennant and all of Fabian's Bay.

In 1879, the work started here, likely on specifications based on outdated data. It was a big job with crowds gathering to watch the estimated 300 men working around the clock, along with the men were some steam navvies and a crane grab.

A dock building type culture emerged, involving things such as coffee shanties and even a meeting house was provided for all the workers for them to conduct any religious activities and services.

This new dock was opened on 18 October 1881. Named the Prince of Wales Dock it was officially opened by the future King Edward VII and Queen Alexandra. Many locals turned out for the event opening. It took until June 1882 for the dock to be ready for shipping.

The first ship to use this dock was a scrap metal vessel called the *Atlas*.

In 1898, an extension increased the capacity, leading it to be one of the biggest in Britain. It allowed Swansea to export tinplate directly to the United States, instead of it having to go via Liverpool.

By 1913, Swansea was shipping out more tinplate and black plate than any other port worldwide.

Other items that passed through these docks included pig iron, timber and pit props.

Coal left via the northern quay. The coal hoists were removed in 1987 and then by 2006 when the docks SA1 transformation was in full swing, the Prince of Wales Dock only received an occasional visit from the city of Cardiff's dredger with sand for United Marine Aggregates.

While industry was booming and steamships becoming even bigger, Swansea found itself yet again in need of more dock space.

In 1904, King Edward VII was back in Swansea to lift the first sod on the foreshore of the Kings Dock.

A part of Swansea Bay was reclaimed to build another dock that would open in 1909 enabling a lot more capacity for the Port of Swansea.

The Queens Dock that had been opened by Queen Mary provided a much-needed boost to the post war fortunes due to its facilities to pump oil directly to and from the refinery.

At the peak of Swansea's maritime heyday, it bore witness to scores of vessels sitting in the bay awaiting their entry into the port.

With Llandarcy's crude oil imports being transferred to Milford Haven via a pipeline connecting the two places, the Queens Dock started to decline.

Around the area of SA1, you can spot some historic buildings, one of my favourites being the Norwegian Church. I not only love the history of this building, and the wonderful people connected to it, but I also like the architecture with its white walls and black peaked roof. In my opinion, a delightful-looking building.

The church, having originally been at Newport, was moved to Swansea in 1910 to a site at the entrance to the docks so that the sailors from Norway had a place for religious services.

After being dismantled again, once it fell out of use, it was rebuilt on a site in the heart of SA1 and is now being used as a nursery.

Another interesting story connected to the docks and the River Tawe, particularly the North Dock, is the story of Swansea Jack. As much a symbol of Swansea as the docks or Kilvey Hill, Swansea Jack was a dog, but not just any dog; he was rather remarkable.

In 1979 a pub that was on the corner of what are now named West and Oystermouth Roads, changed its name in honour of Swansea's four-legged hero.

Jack was a black Labrador Retriever. It is often assumed that the nickname for Swansea people, 'Jacks', as due to this heroic pup, however

I have been told that in a number of areas of Britain the term 'Jack' was applied to sailors, and it's not a far stretch to believe that due to the recognition Swansea waters were receiving, that the nickname could have originated from there.

Jack began his life just as a regular dog, living with his owner William Thomas in accommodation at Padley Yard, North Dock.

Apparently, Jack was initially water shy, and his owner, in an attempt to change this, supposedly threw his young retriever into the North Dock. It appears to have worked as Jack made his first recorded rescue in June 1931.

He saved a twelve-year-old boy who could not swim. He had fallen into the dock and was at great risk of drowning. Jack is said to have thrown himself into the water and pulled the boy to the dockside.

This was just one of many rescues by Jack, including a drunken sailor in the dock, a swimmer who got into trouble in the bay and even a sackful of puppies that had been cruelly tossed in the River Tawe to drown.

Jack quickly went from a top Swansea star to an international canine hero. He made headlines in *The Daily Mirror*; he went on tours; he had a guest spot at Crufts; and was awarded a number of honorary diplomas, medals, cups, tankards, trophies and collars. He was awarded the National Canine Defence League bronze medal twice.

Following Jack's earlier achievements, William Thomas quit Padley Yard in 1933 and stayed for a couple of years at the Victoria Hotel in College Street. William retired from the haulage business in 1936 and moved to live with his daughter and family at Roger Street in the Swansea suburb of Treboeth, and of course Jack went in tow.

But sadly, in September of 1937 Jack fell ill. The vet diagnosed him with delayed phosphorus poisoning, that would have been caused by the accidental ingesting of a poison called Rodine. The poison had slowly eroded the poor dog's organs. On 2 October Jack passed away and a devastated William Thomas wrapped him up in a blanket and buried him.

Shortly after Jack's death a campaign began in the press to find Swansea's cherished canine hero a more honourable final resting place. Eventually the council agreed to rebury Jack on Swansea's promenade. A local undertaker constructed a coffin for him and the heroic dog spent a day or so in the parlour room at 3 Rodger Street surrounded by mementos of his great heroism and flowers. A number of mourners are said to have come to pay their respects.

Nearly a year later on the anniversary of the dog's death, a monument to Jack was unveiled. The stone monument that marks his grave site by the seafront, opposite St Helen's sports ground reads as follows:

> Erected to the memory of Swansea Jack
> The brave retriever who saved 27 human and 2 canine lives
> from drowning
> Loved and mourned by all dog lovers
> Died October 2nd 1937 at the age of seven years
> Neer had mankind more faithful friend
> Than thou
> Who oft thy life didst lend
> To save some human soul from death
> Owner and trainer W.M. Thomas.

There is a bust of a dog's head on the plaque, that is said not to be directly of Jack himself, but of one of his offspring who was considered to closely resemble the famous Jack.

Back to the North Dock for a second and how it has been lost to us, and hence another reason I believe that it is so important to record and keep history alive. For what was once a bustling dock is now filled in and is the site of Parc Tawe, which is a development of retail spaces, cinema, bowling, eateries and Plantasia Zoo. But how many people know whilst choosing their new trainers at Sports Direct just how much history they are standing on?

Commercially speaking the Port of Swansea now consists of only two docks: the Kings Dock and the Queens Dock.

While the South Dock and the Prince of Wales Dock physically still exist, their purpose has changed.

An interview with ex Swansea Dock worker Geoff Deakin

What is your name, age and where were you born?

My full name is Geoffrey Francis Deakin, and I am eighty-two years of age. I was born on 2 February in 1942, during the Second World War. I was born in a house on Oxford Street in Swansea.

What was your family background like? What did your parents do?

I was born into a working-class family. My father's name was Thomas Francis Deakin, and my mother's name was Olwen Annie Deakin, with her maiden name being Owen.

My father worked as a crane-driver on Swansea Docks. He started working there in 1937, while my mother was a shop assistant and short-hand typist.

What was your first job and when did you begin working at Swansea Docks?

I worked firstly as an apprentice in a garage until I was nineteen years of age, before being employed by Swansea Docks in 1961 as a crane-driver. In those days if your Dad worked there, you had a good chance of being employed as well.

What part of the docks did you work in and what duties did you have?

I was stationed at the Kings Dock as a crane-driver, which involved the loading and unloading of cargo from the ships. I worked there for thirty years in total. I was paid on tonnage, so the busier they were, the more I was able to earn. If they did not have the boats in and were quiet, we would be paid the minimum wage of the time.

What was a typical day like for you, working on the docks?

A typical working day was 7am to 4.30pm and my working week would run from Monday to Friday. If it was a quiet day, you would be sent home early.

What were the advantages and disadvantages of working at Swansea Docks?

An advantage of working there was being able to work outdoors, but then again, that was not so good when you were 60-70 foot high in your crane when bad weather could set in such as the wind and the rain.

Another advantage of working on the docks was the early finishes, but of course that was then met with the disadvantage of not earning good money.

Above and below: Walking around St Thomas and Port Tennant in Swansea, seeing some of the last remaining working docks of Swansea in the distance.

CHAPTER EIGHT

One of my Favourite Finds

One of my absolute all-time favourite finds was upon Carreg Coch Mountain in the Brecon Beacons.

To paint a picture, Wales is home to the stunning Brecon Beacons, a paradise and sanctuary to walkers through these Welsh hills.

However, this amazing gentle landscape of rolling hills, has a darker side that can quickly reveal itself when the weather changes. The weather here can change on a dime. It can become an extremely harsh and unforgiving environment, the Jekyll and Hyde of landscapes if you like.

But due to this, as a walker, explorer or adventurer you must take care, wear appropriate clothing and footwear, check weather conditions, be sensible and prepared for all eventualities.

This is also the main reason why the area is littered with the wreckage of World War aircraft as the air force conducted training exercises in this area due to its unforgiving nature to prepare pilots and crews for war.

Many accidents occurred in the area of the Beacons and sadly a lot of fatalities took place. Some of the crash sites are marked by items such as memorial stones or plaques bearing the names of the men who had tragically died there.

Today at all of these crash sites, there is little to no evidence of wreckages; they stay alive in old maps or grid references and stories.

One of my Favourite Finds

I have often visited this area and on one planned occasion, I was told about a Wellington Bomber crash site on Carreg Coch; interestingly there was still a lot of the plane remaining, marked by a memorial to the crew who were all tragically killed along with a large Canadian flag marking the spot.

I also discovered that although this wreckage still sits amongst the Beacons, it's been said that it is starting to disappear little-by-little, as some people visiting the area are taking mementoes with them. Something that I disagree with.

With my interest peaked, I began my research, and we visited Carreg Coch.

The photograph was taken at Carreg Coch and depicts the crash site of a Wellington Bomber aircraft from the Second World War, along with a poppy wreath laid as a tribute to its crew.

However, this plane wreckage took us three attempts to actually locate, and as I've previously stated, nature is a law unto herself, and even in good weather conditions, the further you climb in the Brecon Beacons the colder and windier it can become. But I was determined to find it having put the effort in to climbing this mountain, so we returned.

Carreg Coch, I found to be a tough climb. I found it a very untouched, natural place. On one visit we took a wrong turn and found ourselves near very soggy, boggy ground and on the first visit we must have detoured on the way back down and as a result for the last bit, we had to walk down a very steep grassy bank. That was not planned.

So please be careful visiting here. Of course it is important to be careful visiting any mountain but compared with somewhere such as Pen y Fan (also found in the Brecon Beacons), that is very well-known and has well-trodden paths from many a walking boot, Carreg Coch sees very little activity. For example, on an individual visit, I would probably have been able to count the other people I saw there on one hand.

Standing on Carreg Coch we looked out at a sea of green and grey stone. I find this magnificent, majestic and magical.

As I stated at the start of this book, being a natural overthinker, I find moments like this good for my mindset and find them very calming. A natural therapy if you like.

But I'm getting sidetracked now, back to the Wellington Bomber. Our third climb was successful in finding the plane, though I have to admit even though we tried to work it out via maps, grid references and coordinates, in the end it came down to luck.

Picture two very tired, deflated hikers, thinking they would never actually find this important piece of history.

We had come across two other hikers and I asked them did they know if we were anywhere near the site of the Wellington Bomber, but they had no idea that a plane wreckage was even up there. So we carried on climbing, and then later on by pure fluke we saw another two walkers along with their dog. We tried yet again this time, expecting the same response, however we were met with 'yes we know that, in fact we've just been there'. Our faces could not contain our excitement and with a renewed energy and enthusiasm we eagerly followed the directions we were given.

One of my Favourite Finds

After a short distance, we sat there against a most beautiful backdrop of the wreckage of the Wellington Bomber, with the red-and-white Canadian flag sombrely blowing with the breeze.

It was a lovely day, and the contrast of spectacular scenery, dazzling in the sunshine compared to the cold grey metal laying broken on the floor was distinctive.

We were both relieved to have finally found it, but also deeply saddened by the quick reality of what happened here, for a few moments I was at a loss for words.

On the night of 20 November 1944, Wellington Bomber MF509 was on an exercise, but due to engine issues, causing it to fly into clouds that in turn caused an ice build-up, the plane crashed into Carreg Coch killing all aboard.

The Canadian flag that has been placed at the site of a Wellington bomber wreckage in memory of its crew.

Walking Welsh History: A History of South and Mid-Wales on Foot

A wreath at the Wellington Bomber site.

The wreckage site of the Wellington Bomber against the beautiful green backdrop.

One of my Favourite Finds

A close-up photograph of the Wellington Bomber wreckage demonstrating the destruction of the sad event.

Time doesn't stand still, the top half of the photo shows sunshine on a beautiful day, while the bottom of the photograph shows a brutal grey plane wreckage of the past.

Bibliography

Brookes, G. 2013 *Swansea Murders*. The History Press.
Draisey, D. 2010 *The Rebecca Riots Within Ten Miles of Swansea*. Draisey Publishing.
Evans, C. and Miskell, L. 2020 *Swansea Copper*. Johns Hopkins University Press.
Gwynn, D. 2019 *Lost Swansea*. Amberley Publishing.
Inman, M. L. 2017 *Swansea Docks in the 1960s*. Amberley Publishing.
Innes-Smith, R. 1996 *Pembroke Castle: Birthplace of the Tudor Dynasty*. Heritage House group Ltd – New edition.
Jenkins, N. 2008 *Real Swansea*. Seren Illustrated edition.
Kenyon, J. R. 2003 *Raglan Castle*. Cadw Welsh Historic Monument Rev Ed.
McLees, D. 2005 *Discover Castell Coch*. Cadw Welsh Historic Monuments Rev Ed.
Miskell, L. (ed.) 2010 *Robert Morris and the First Swansea Copper Works c. 1727–1730*. South Wales Record Society.
Owen, R. 2023 *Castles of Wales*. Graffeg Limited.
Phillips, A. 2014 *Castles of Wales*. Stroud: Amberley Publishing.
Rees, S. E. and Caple, C. 2007 *Dinefwr Castle, Dryslwyn Castle*. Cadw Welsh Historic Monuments.
Robins, N. A. 2023 *Cilfái Historical Geography on Kilvey Hill, Swansea*. Nyddfwch.
Stevens, C. 2006 *The Rebecca Riots*. Gomer Press.

Bibliography

Turner, R. 2016 *Discover Caerphilly Castle*. Cadw Welsh Historic Monuments.
Turner, R. 2002: revised ed 2010 *Discover Chepstow Castle*. Cadw Welsh Historic Monuments.

Websites

'Muriel Drinkwater'. Available at: http://www.bbc.co.uk
'Dylan Thomas'. Available at: Beamingnotes.com
'Dylan Thomas'. Available at: http://www.britannica.com
'Dylan Thomas'. Available at: Discoverdylanthomas.com
'Dylan Thomas birthplace number 5 Cwmdonkin Drive birthplace and family home of Dylan Thomas' Available at: dylanThomasbirthplace.com
'Dylan Thomas'. Available at: https://www.theguardian.com
'The unsolved murder of Muriel Drinkwater'. Available at: https://www.herald.wales
'Elizabeth Melville article (Muriel Drinkwater)'. Available at: Medium.com
Penllergaer Forest. Available at: Melinlian.net
'Dylan Thomas'. Available at: Poets.org
Swansea and the Industrial Revolution Copperopolis' and 'Morfa Copperworks'. Available at: http://www.swanseamuseum.co.uk
'Muriel Joan Drinkwater'. Available at: Unsolvedmurders.co.uk
'Take a tour of Dylan Thomas' Laugharne'. Available at: http://www.visitwales.com
'The unsolved murder of 12-year-old Muriel Drinkwater and the new suspect identified'. Available at Walesonline.co.uk
Identity of 1946 schoolgirl murderer remains a mystery after DNA left on her 'little red riding hood' coat fails to link to child killer suspected of being notorious Jack the Stripper: available at: dailymail.com

Documentary

BBC. Darkland: Hunting the Killers, Series 1, Episode 3: 'Muriel Drinkwater'.
Secrets of Great British Castle – season 2: episode 2: Cardiff.

Index

Aberystwyth 100
Anglesey 124, 132

Beaufort, Duke of 129, 176
Bethell, Paul 20, 24, 25
Bigod, Roger 47, 50
Booth, Richard 105, 106
Brecon Beacons 186, 189
Bruges, William 37, 39-43
Brown, Lancelot Capability 96, 99
Browns Hotel 14
Burges, William 67
Burrell, Freda 24
Bute, Fifth Marquess of 38, 42
Bute, Lady 42, 43
Bute, Second Marquess of 37
Bute, Third Marquess of (see also *Crichton-Stuart, John Patrick*) 37, 39-42
Buzzy, Mansell 129

Caerphilly 34
Caerphilly Castle 34, 40, 41, 43, 52-63, 69, 106
Cardiff 32, 49, 64, 169, 182
Cardiff Castle 32-38, 65, 68, 109
Carreg Coch 186-189
Castell Coch 38-43, 68
Charles I 50, 51, 66, 82, 83
Chapel, J. S. 42
Chepstow Castle 45-52, 60, 80, 81
Chile 125, 140-141
Cilgerran Castle 101-104
Cornwall 123, 124, 145
Coster, Thomas 129
Crichton-Stuart, John Patrick 39
Cromwell, Oliver 74, 84, 101
Cuba 125
Curthose, Robert 34
Cwmdonkin Park 2, 6-10

Index

Dark, Colin 24, 25
Darby, Neil 24
Dafydd ap Gruffudd 91
Deakin, Geoff 183, 184
de Bohun, Humphrey 56, 57
de Clare, Eleanor 62, 63, 65
de Clare, Gilbert 34, 46, 53-59, 69, 73, 88, 100
de Clare, Isabella 46, 47
de Clare, Richard 46, 53
de Valence, William 72
Despenser, Hugh 35, 36, 93
Despenser the Elder, Hugh 63, 64
Despenser the Younger, Hugh 49, 62-65
Disraeli, Benjamin 39, 40
Drinkwater, Muriel 17-30
Drinkwater, Percy 17, 20, 28
Drinkwater, Margaret 17, 20
Dryslwyn Castle 85-88, 90-94, 96, 97, 99, 100
Dinefwr Castle 85-94, 109, 110

Edward I 48, 49, 63, 88, 90, 91, 92
Edward II 11, 35, 36, 49, 57, 60, 64, 93
Edward III 103
Edward IV 80, 81
Edward VI 36

Fern Hill 3, 8
Fitzhamon, Robert 34
FitzOsbern, William 34
Frame, William 42, 68

Glyndŵr, Owain 35, 36, 49, 65, 77, 94, 100, 103
Gowerton 17
Greg, Rhys 87, 88
Grenfell, Pascoe 133, 135, 137, 138
Grenfell, William 137
Grenfell family 117
Gruffudd ap Rhys 56, 60

Harries, John 26-28
Harries, Phoebe 26-28
Harries, Ronald 26-28
Hafod Copperworks 131, 133, 134, 136, 147, 151, 153
Hay castle 105, 106
Hafod Morfa 157, 158, 160
Henry I 34, 45, 46, 78, 103
Henry II 46, 70-72, 86, 100, 104
Henry III 47, 54-56, 88, 90
Henry IV 36, 65
Henry VI 73, 76, 78, 96
Henry VII 73, 74, 96
Henry VIII 49, 50, 79, 81, 100, 103
Henry Tudor 49, 79-81, 96
Herbert, Henry 51, 66
Herbert, Walter 80, 81
Herbert, William 36, 49
Hoyles, Hubert 20, 23, 25

Isabella of France 49, 64
Isabella, Queen 35, 36, 64, 65

Jones, Harold 23-26
Jones, John 163-164, 172, 173

Killick, Vera 12
Killick, William 12
Kilvey Hill 113-122, 181

Laugharne 2-3, 10-16, 100
Lane, John 125, 127, 128
le Play, Fredic 143, 145, 147
Llywelyn Bren 35, 36, 60, 62
Llywelyn ap Gruffudd 48, 53, 54-58, 89, 90
Llywelyn ap Iorwerth 55, 71, 88, 100, 103
Little, Florence 24
London 2-3, 26, 27, 39, 132, 169, 172
Lloyd George, David 20
Lundgren, Sam 24

Majoda 12
Maelgwyn ap Rhys 87, 88, 100
Marshal, Anslem 47, 72, 103
Marshal, Richard 72
Marshal, Walter 47
Marshal, William 46, 47, 70-72, 103
Martin, Sheila 26, 29
Middle Bank Copperworks 115, 131-133, 137, 145, 147-149, 153, 155
de Montfort, Simon 53-55
Morfa Copper Works 131, 137, 155
Mortimer, Roger 36, 54, 64, 65

Napier, Captain 164-167, 169, 170, 171
Nazis 37, 38, 119

Newquay, Wales 2, 11, 12
Newton House 95-99

Osbern, Fitz 44, 45

Pascoe, Grenfell 117, 133, 135, 137, 138
Pembroke Castle 47, 69-71, 108, 109
Pendine 26
Penllergaer 17-31, 119, 170
Percival, Joseph 129, 132
Pollard, Paul 125
Popkin, Thomas 127, 128, 145
Pontraddulais 162-165

Raglan Castle 76-79, 85, 106
Rebecca Riots 151, 161-174
Rhys ap Maredudd 90-92
Rhys Mechyll 88, 89
Rhys Fychan 89, 90
Rhys Ieuanc 87, 88
Rhys Wyndod 90, 91
Rhys ap Thomas 96
Rhys ap Tewdwr 103
Rhys ap Gruffudd 86-88, 94
Richard I 46, 47
Rufus, William 34

Second World War 4, 68, 119
Sheila, Martin 26, 29
Swansea Docks 175-185
Swansea Jack 181-183

Tircoed Forest Village 17, 29
Thomas, Caitlin 3, 4, 10-13

Index

Thomas, David John 3, 13
Thomas, Dylan 1-16, 100
Thomas, Florence Hannah 3, 13
Thomas, Ivy and Ebie 11, 14
Townsend, Chauncy 132
Tudor, Jasper 73, 78, 79
Tudor, Owain 73
Tyle Du Farm 17

Under Milk Wood 1, 11, 14
Upper Bank Copper Works 131, 132, 145
Uplands, Swansea 2-6

Vivian, H. H. 155
Vivian, John 133-134, 147, 149
Vivian, John Henry 117, 133, 152, 178
Vivian, Richard Hussey 136
Vivian and Sons 134, 135, 155, 156, 158

Wallace, William 48, 77-80
White Rock 116, 117, 129, 131, 132, 145, 151, 155, 157
William, Frame 37
William the Conqueror 32, 34, 44-45
Williams Foster & Co 154, 156, 157
Winch Room, Castell Coch 43
Wogan's Cavern 76, 109